REVIEWERS' COMMENTS

"Professor Hinrichs has written an elegant, taut, and well-reasoned discussion of film as art. Does modern film qualify as art—or at least as good art? Professor Hinrichs poses this question, then in a treatment that is balanced, fair, and impeccably argued, he presents both sides of this controversy in this insightful and provocative book."

— Professor Gary R. Evans
Harvey Mudd College

"After reading this book, you will never see films in the same way again. Professor Hinrichs takes the film industry to task for its formulaic approach to filmmaking. He challenges our visual aesthetics and teaches us to become more informed, critical viewers. This book is a significant contribution and an important source for anyone interested in film as art."

— Robert Toensing, Professor of Art
Anoka-Ramsey Community College

"Informative, provocative, artful. Topics are treated with admirable scope and engaging detail. Hinrichs' fresh, vivid style, adroit incorporation of marvelous quotations, and clear presentation make this an excellent and inspiring introduction to the art of film."

—Lynn Greenberg
Professor of Philosophy and Humanities
Century College

"Excellent! Professor Hinrichs has succeeded in a most difficult task, sorting through and condensing a massive amount of information in a way that is exceptionally useful and engaging. *Film & Art* is a great introduction to how to think about film in a creative and critical way."

— Bruce Mamer
author of *Film Production Technique:
Creating the Accomplished Image*

Also by Bruce H. Hinrichs:

Mind as Mosaic: The Robot in the Machine

(J - Press, 2000)

Film

&

Art

by

Bruce H. Hinrichs

First j-Press paperback printing, 1999
Second j-Press paperback printing, 2000
Third j-Press paperback printing, 2002

Cover art and design by Nicole Hinrichs-Bideau

Editing and photographic illustrations by Bruce H. Hinrichs

Printed in the United States of America

ISBN: 0-9660111-2-0

Library of Congress catalog card number: 99-64630

The cover: The images on the cover illustrate one of this book's major themes, that film has at times been a medium of artistic excellence, revelation and splendor, on a par with other art forms. On the front cover, metaphorically floating on a screen of white light, are two enlarged frames from the marvelous and enigmatic landmark film, *The Blood of a Poet* (1930), made by the French creative genius Jean Cocteau, whose films are unique masterpieces of artistic style and substance, innovative and poetic, startling and sublime. They are pristine examples of moments from cinematic history that ultimately achieved the kind of ecstatic or poetic truth that is discussed in Chapter Six, Cognition and Meaning: The Illumination of Truth. These images illustrate film's ability to transcend narration, fiction, or simple facts, and to ascend to a higher aesthetic plane that helps to cultivate and illuminate the truths that touch, propel, and enrich our lives.

On the back cover is an image of the creation of the robot woman from the masterpiece *Metropolis* (1926), one of history's most influential and captivating films. This enduring expressionist film was directed by Fritz Lang, an architect of the screen and an artist of composition and style, whose films always carried with them a true and moral sense and demonstrated unforgettable imagery that is only possible in the cinema. This image exemplifies the theme of this book that the film medium has at times created its own artistic styles, motifs, and structures, that the grammar of film and its visual choreography are singular within the domain of the arts, and that the cinema can at times, in certain rare moments, be rightfully appreciated as a worthy artistic endeavor and an illuminating contributor to our understanding of ourselves, our world, our circumstances, our relationships, and the human condition.

For Nicole and Danielle

ACKNOWLEDGMENTS

*T*hanks to such masters of the cinema as Bergman, Lang, Resnais, Godard, Cocteau, and so many others whose films inspired my study of the cinema. Thanks to my many fantastic and challenging students. Thanks to my outstanding colleagues at Century College. Thanks to Bruce Mamer, Gary Evans, Lynn Greenberg, and Bob Toensing for reviewing the manuscript. Thanks to Ellen Collopy for help in editing, support, and friendship. Thanks to Danielle Hinrichs for encouragement, the inspiration to write, and the desire to write well, to Nicole Hinrichs-Bideau for her aesthetic sensibilities, for motivating me to study film, and for the scintillating design of this book's cover. Finally, thanks to my editor and publisher, Sid Jackson, who made this book possible.

*"Thanks to art, instead of seeing a single world, our own, we see it
multiply until we have before us as many worlds as there are original
artists."*
— *Marcel Proust*

CONTENTS

INTRODUCTION

*"They have imposed on us with their pale half-fledged protestations,
trembling about in inarticulate frenzy, saying it is not for us to
understand art..."*
— Marianne Moore

*F*ilm has been called the art of the twentieth century. Born in
1895, the cinema is now more than one hundred years old and
it seems an appropriate time to ask to what extent film has lived
up to that optimistic pronouncement. Is film an art form, and if
so, what kind, what styles, and what quality of art has it produced?
Which films and filmmakers of the past century represent the best of the
art? To what extent has the cinema achieved its potential as a unique,
multi-dimensional, multi-faceted art form?

The cinema in many ways borrows from and overlaps with all
other art forms, such as painting, photography, dance, music, theater, literature, poetry, and even architecture. Yet film is an art unto itself
because, like no other art medium, the cinema records movement. In
this sense, the cinema is a part of the other arts, yet still stands on its
own.

The cinema stands apart from the other arts in still another
important way. It is far and away the most commercial of all the arts
and thereby the most subject to mass tastes and popular appeal. This
fact has repressed and strangled the artistic side of film because the
movie industry is now unrelentingly controlled by the forces of the marketplace and by business decisions (i.e., profits). Modern movies are
not made by artists, they are made by accountants. Our mass media per-
petuates this system because it is profitable. This, of course, means that
to a large extent the cinema has failed in its role as an art form. It has
become a commercial part of the popular culture, a component of mass-
market entertainment similar to television, toys, cartoons, comic books,
and video games, rather than a means of artistic expression and communication.

Perhaps this unfortunate result was inevitable because of the
enormous expense of making a film and the seemingly limitless greed
for profits, or because of the power that film has as a tool of mass entertainment, or because of the nature of the cinema's mode of exhibition (a
mall, rather than a museum) and the type of audience that it attracts.
Whatever the reasons, in its brief one hundred year history, film has pro-

gressively become more and more a commercial component of mass culture and less and less an artistic medium exhibiting depth, experimentation, and enlightening ideas.

In spite of the great shortcomings of the film medium, in spite of its use as a mass entertainment vehicle, it can be argued that there have been a fair number of artistic successes in film's one hundred years of existence. Throughout the past century the cinema has provided some uniquely profound, singularly inimitable pieces of art. Certain filmmakers have risen above the mundane, above the cynical commercial landscape of the movie industry, and have sculpted beautiful masterpieces of film artistry. Amid the banal and tasteless majority of movies (just as would be found in any other art medium, it well might be said), there exist paragons of the medium, films that exemplify the best and the most honest attempts at artistic expression.

Unlike many other art forms, film is global in its influence. The great early filmmaker and scholar Sergei Eisenstein noted that "The cinema is undoubtedly the most international of all arts." It is international not only in its viewership, but also in the production of films. Although Oscar Wilde quipped that "Art never expresses anything but itself," his claim does not seem true of the cinema. Film art seems to have an ability perhaps beyond any other of the arts to express social and cultural values and ideas from the far corners of the globe. Despite the expense and the planning and coordination that are required, glorious films are made around the world in even some of the poorest and most unsettled countries. In fact, sometimes hardships contribute to creating the best, most profound art. As the character Harry Lime says in *The Third Man* (1949), "In Italy for thirty years they had warfare, terror, murder, bloodshed—they produced Michelangelo, Leonardo da Vinci, and the Renaissance. In Switzerland they had brotherly love, five hundred years of democracy, and peace—and what did they produce? The cuckoo clock."

To what extent is film an art form and to what extent has it succeeded in portraying truth and illuminating audiences? This book is an attempt to define and evaluate the film medium as an art form, to put film into its place among the other arts. The reader is invited to explore the history of film, its terminology, structure, and its techniques, and to evaluate in what ways film has fulfilled its potentials and in what ways it has failed. The cinema has been with us for some time now, but has it matured? To what extent does filmdom represent the highest quality and integrity of artistic expression and communication?

In an attempt to address this issue, this book is divided into three parts. The first part, "Thinking About Film," is meant primarily as motivational and preliminary, to present a foundation for thinking about film as an art form. The first three chapters provide some ideas about the study of films, the viewing of films, and tips for analyzing and evaluating films. The intent in the first section is to motivate the reader to think more seriously and more critically about film and its standing among the arts.

The second part of this volume, "Understanding Film," focuses on the nature of film—its history, its structure, its physical form, and the meanings that it conveys. The reader is invited to become familiar with film history, terminology, structure, film's various genres and styles, and to begin to understand the nature of its production and exhibition. This second section also deals with the importance of the film viewer's cognitive processes and the meanings that are thereby derived from films. It is argued here that the meanings that are conveyed by a work of art are the most critical ingredients for making a proper evaluation of the art's worth.

The third and final section of this book, "Appraising Film as Art," tackles the various issues that arise when we conceptualize film as an art form, and presents a discussion of the cinema's successes and failures in that regard. Film is discussed in the context of the other arts—naturally with respect to the past one hundred years, which means the period of Modern and Post-Modern artistic and literary styles—and with regard to the corresponding aesthetic theories and principles of Modern art. The reader will find arguments both for and against the cinema as a successful art form. Many examples of films are provided, all of which are recommended for viewing and which were selected with the assumption that the vast majority of these films can be fairly easily located at local video stores.

Throughout the book, important terms are in bold print, and definitions can be found in the glossary at the back of the book. A number of appendices are also included at the end of the text that will provide useful reference information in a tabular or list form. Also, at the end of this volume the reader will find a bibliography of important and influential film and art books and an index to this volume.

It is my hope that this book will help readers learn more about film as an art, that they will find it enjoyable, informative, and thought provoking, and that this book conveys the excitement, joy, and enlightenment film and the other arts can provide. It is my intent that this volume will awaken in the reader some thoughts, some motivation, and some interest in the issues, facts, and ideas presented.

Finally, I aspire to the sentiment of the great existentialist author Franz Kafka who wrote, "A book must be the axe for the frozen sea inside us." To whatever extent that this book can be an axe for the reader's frozen sea, I will be most pleased and gratified.

Bruce H. Hinrichs
Minneapolis, Minnesota
1999

PART ONE

Thinking

About

Film

*"Conception, my boy, fundamental brainwork, is what makes
the difference in all art."*
— Dante Gabriel Rossetti

*M*ost of us simply take movies for granted and talk about them in ways that rarely address the more profound and aesthetic details of their technical, artistic, social, or philosophical aspects. When we talk about films we say what we like or don't like, how they make us feel, which scenes and characters we remember and who we liked and who we didn't like, and what we would have done in their place, what mistakes and discontinuities we noticed in the production, and especially, whether we thought a film was realistic or not. It is assumed that an unrealistic film is a bad film.

If we are asked what a film is about, we relate only the story, as if we were talking about a book. We never mention technique or style, as we might if we were asked about a painting or a sculpture, or even about a poem. How can we begin to take film as an art more seriously, to begin to think and talk about the medium in a more sophisticated and detailed manner?

The first three chapters of this book are meant to inspire and to motivate you to think more seriously and deeply about films, particularly films as art. The first chapter deals with some preliminaries, introducing and describing the various categories involved in the study of film.

The second chapter presents some ideas about how to watch a film more critically, how to become more aware of what is happening on the screen and how and why it is happening, and why the film is having the effect on you that it is. To become a critical viewer of film—of any art form—requires some work, some concentration, and some different ways of looking and thinking, but it is well worth the effort because the result is that a whole new, exciting world will be opened up to you.

The final chapter in this first section, chapter three, provides some ideas about how to analyze and talk about films. This is a large topic, of course, and would easily fill a multi-volume set of books, so naturally the subject is only briefly introduced here.

It is hoped that these chapters will provide a good starting point for you to become more serious about films and about art in general, that they will motivate you to learn more about art and film, that they will whet your appetite for more information and ideas, and that they will provide some rich insights and hints about how better to think about film and art.

Chapter One

FILM STUDIES
The Magic of the Light

"Life demands a passion."
— *Jorge Luis Borges*

"Even a thought, even a possibility, can shatter us and transform us."
— *Friedrich Nietzsche*

A trip to the movies is one of the most shared experiences in our culture. Perhaps that is why we are so nonchalant about it. From near and far, as individuals, families, dates, or friends, we sporadically file into a movie theater, there to gradually merge into an audience. The house lights dim, the projector light bursts onto the screen, and we are one on a journey of sounds and images.

The movies have endured in pretty much the same format for over one hundred years. In that time audiences have reacted to them and continue to react with deep emotions and vigorous discussions. How often have we sat in that darkened theater and lost ourselves in the flickering light? We have snuggled and kissed, laughed and screamed, and oh, how we have cried! Once I even fell out of my seat laughing so hard at a Woody Allen film that I found myself almost literally rolling in the aisle!

The movies have been an integral part of our lives and a rich reservoir of memories and references. They have influenced our ideas about heroes, morality, justice, romance, adventure, and nearly every other aspect of life. When we realize the importance of the movies, it becomes apparent that film study is a worthy and serious undertaking.

In the Beginning

How did it all begin? A funny thing about the invention of movies: it didn't happen all at once. Movies as we know them today resulted from a gradual evolution. There was no one single event that marks the definitive invention of the cinema. Motion pictures evolved from a series of disparate but converging ideas, devices, people, and circumstances over many years, finally culminating in the late nineteenth century in the form with which we are familiar today.

Robertson's Fantasmagorie (what a great name!) was just one of the celebrated **magic lanterns** of the eighteenth and nineteenth centuries. These devices were the first to contain light source, image, and projecting lens all in one unit, similar to a slide projector. Illusionists would travel the countryside with their magic lanterns strapped to their backs, and at show time would present a series of images (ghosts and demons were popular) projected onto walls, sheets, or even onto billows of smoke, which must have produced an eerie sight.

Motion toys, consisting of images on strips of paper which when viewed while spinning produced the illusion of movement, with such exotic and exquisite names as the Phenakistoscope, the Thaumatrope, and the Zoetrope (literally, wheel of life; a name later adopted by Francis Ford Coppola for his production company), were based on a principle of perception called **persistence of vision**. The eye will retain an image in memory for a very brief period, a split second, after seeing it. A similar effect is the **phi phenomenon**. If two lights placed close together are alternately turned on and off rapidly enough, a viewer will perceive motion—one light appears to be moving back and forth. If the lights are different colors, then to the viewer one light appears to jump back and forth but switch color in the middle where in fact there is no light at all! These simple demonstrations unveil the startling fact that our world of experience is largely created in our mind. Peter Mark Roget (of *Roget'sThesaurus* fame) in 1824 was the first to suggest that because of these principles a very rapid sequence of images will give the perception of motion. You have probably experienced this effect by fanning pages in front of your eyes, each page containing a picture slightly different from the last.

The modern cinema, of course, is dependent on the same principles. The amazing fact is that a motion picture does not show motion; rather, the movement is perceived by the viewer. A series of still frames flashed quickly before the eye (usually today at a rate of twenty-four frames per second) creates the perceptual effect—a motion picture. So it seems movies are illusions in more ways than one might have thought.

Three landmark events led to the cinema in its present form. In 1888, George Eastman developed a light-sensitive paper on a roll, which he called "film." Soon afterward, William Dickson, a British employee of Thomas Edison, developed a sprocket mechanism for the vertical advancement of a roll of film that he had perforated. Finally, French brothers Louis and Auguste Lumière, who ran a photographic equipment company in Lyons, invented the Cinematographe, a machine capable of recording images on film and then later projecting the frames in rapid succession onto a large screen.

It was on March 10, 1895 when the Lumière brothers first used their hand-cranked Cinematographe to project images from film to screen. Then on December 28, 1895, in Paris, the brothers treated a paying audience to the first public showing of films. Now, more than one hundred years later, we still gather in front of a screen to experience the magic of the light.

Getting Serious

Film study can be fun, informative, useful, rewarding, and a rich component of your personal and intellectual development. Film study is becoming increasingly popular and important. It is related to many aspects of our culture—such as the emphasis on the visual presentation of information through television, computers, and print—and can be an exceedingly interesting and illuminating subject.

The study of films is naturally a young discipline compared to most, but has advanced a good deal more than most people realize. There is not much publicity for serious cinema studies. If you announce that you are going to take a film class, most people assume that means you will be sitting around watching movies and then discussing them. While this is sometimes the case, film studies can be much more rigorous and theoretical. In fact, there are levels of film analysis suitable for most everyone.

Though it is still a relatively young field, film study can at times be very serious, difficult, profound, theoretical and scholarly. Many of history's foremost filmmakers and film theorists were intellectual artists whose works greatly influenced many people, institutions, and ideas. Essays and books about the cinema can be esoteric and complicated works of social, historical, and artistic commentary. So, quite unlike a simple evening at the movies, film study is often a serious and difficult enterprise. However, it is also fabulously intriguing and engrossing, and endlessly illuminating in more ways than one.

Visual literacy is a very important part of modern life. Images are everywhere. The use of film, video, and computer multimedia pervades all walks of contemporary society—advertising, politics, business, industry and commerce, sports, education, medicine, and (of course) entertainment. The phenomenon is worldwide. The use of the visual image is universal. Did you know that India produces more films each year than does Hollywood? The Bombay-based industry is known as Bollywood!

Films are only one small part of our visually oriented world. Video production and multimedia are among the fastest growing fields in the world. One asset of cinema study is that a proper understanding of film and the use of visual imagery can provide a useful and significant advantage in many avenues of contemporary life.

Most colleges today offer a variety of courses on the cinema, but this is a very loose subject area, far from being well organized as a discipline. Therefore, courses in film studies vary tremendously from one college to another. Even at a particular school, film courses will likely be spread out among many different academic departments since most colleges do not have one unified department of film studies. Another problem is that there is no widely accepted canon of films within the various cinema studies disciplines. This means that each course you take or book that you read on the cinema will likely cover a wide assortment of different films with only sporadic and coincidental overlap, with a few exceptions.

Here are some of the courses and departments that you are likely to discover in your educational journey through the study of cinema:

History of Film: Very often the study of film is approached from a historical perspective with emphasis on the events that led to the development of the film medium, important films and filmmakers, and the study of cinematic themes that reflected or influenced society. Such courses look at important events that led to the development of the cinema such as the inventions of the late 19th century, like the Kinetoscope, and then normally take a chronological approach covering the silent era, talkies, **film noir**, film genres, and last, the contemporary cinema. Films are typically studied within the context of historical events, such as the Great Depression, the Cold War, the Vietnam War, and the Watergate crisis. These courses also emphasize historical developments like the rise of the studio system, particular themes in films such as gender or ethnicity, and a chronology of significant cinema events, important directors and films, and the emergence of film theories. However, film theory is usually not emphasized in these courses, nor is production or technology.

Film Production: Some colleges and technical institutions offer courses in the filmmaking process, including courses in screenwriting and the technical aspects of using cameras, lighting, sets, props, editing, and so on. Students in these courses typically get very little introduction to film theory, history, film genres, or the art of film. The terminology covered typically centers on technical matters such as camera f-stops, use of proper light fixtures and settings, **rack focusing**, editing principles and techniques, and the like. Students usually use department equipment to make short films, often cooperating in the acting, camera work, and editing of their projects. Students begin working with 8mm or 16mm equipment and develop their skills in **cinematography**, direction, lighting, sets, editing, and the use of sound. Screenwriting courses provide an introduction to the fundamental formats and traditions of writing a screenplay (one page per minute of film, for example) and allow for practice in creative writing within that special format.

The Art of Film: These courses tend to be in the humanities or art history departments. Films are treated as any other art medium and are analyzed primarily according to aesthetic criteria. Just as one would study painting, music, dance, literature, poetry, architecture, sculpture, or any other art, the cinema is examined and evaluated regarding its artistic themes, styles, techniques, and other traditional and academic qualities related to the arts. Typical subject matter includes the interpretation and analysis of **mise-en-scene**, composition, cinematography, lighting, **montage**, and **motifs**. Important directors, such as Sergei Eisenstein, Ingmar Bergman, Alfred Hitchcock, or Federico Fellini, and significant and influential films, such as *The Seventh Seal* (1957), *Citizen Kane* (1941), *Breathless* (1959), or *M* (1931) are studied, just as you would study important

Peter Lorre reflects on his compulsion in *M*

artists and paintings in an art history class. Over-arching qualities of film, such as the use of realism vs. formalism, are often examined. Some courses will lean heavily toward films as literature, others toward film as visual art, and others toward **avant-garde** or experimental films.

<u>Communication and Literature</u>: Many colleges offer film courses through their departments of communication, media studies, comparative literature or English literature. Film courses are often a part of helping students understand cultural ideas and differences, how ideas are communicated, and the effect of different forms of communication—written, oral, or visual for example. Films may be analyzed for their story-telling (**narrative**) qualities, their use of **motifs** or themes, their expression of values, beliefs, archetypes, and traditions, or their depiction of the culture in which they are embedded. These courses tend to be analytical, concentrating on an understanding of cultural and social meanings, subtexts, and connotations of films. Usually these courses require more student discussion and writing than most other film study courses.

<u>Cultural Studies</u>: The study of film is often a means of better understanding a culture or society. Cinema courses are often found in departments of French, Italian, and Russian, for example. Famous culture and art critic, Siegfried Kracauer, pioneered this idea in his 1957 book, *From Caligari to Hitler*. The title refers to a 1919 German film titled *The Cabinet of Dr. Caligari*, which was one of the first films to employ a certain artistic style called **Expressionism**. Often certain styles of film are associated with certain countries and periods of time. For example, Italian **Neorealism** offered a realistic look at post World War II conditions in Italy.

An expressionist set in
The Cabinet of Dr. Caligari

German expressionist films were an artistic form of cinema that emphasized the look of the film and included distorted, expressive sets, movements, lighting, and themes. Their intent was to express the vision and thematic ideas of the filmmaker rather than to replicate reality. These films were very common in the 1920s and influenced filmmaking to this day. Modern filmmaker Tim Burton often used expressionism in such films as *Batman* (1989) and *Edward Scissorhands* (1990).

Expressionism also influenced the style of movies known as **film noir**, which were highly stylized dramas that used high contrast black and white lighting and clipped dialogue in order to portray a world of crime and betrayal.

Kracauer's thesis was that an examination of German expressionist films could provide valuable insight into the psyche of post-WWI German society and might help explain the rise of Hitler and Nazism. This idea became widely adopted as a means of examining film within a cultural context, so that today film studies courses often examine films with respect to social and cultural criteria and events. The thesis of this approach is that analysis of a body of films can tell us about the values of the culture within which they were produced.

Film Departments: Some colleges and universities have departments exclusively devoted to film study. They do not necessarily look at film as art or communication or expression or metaphor, but study the cinema for its own sake, on its own terms. The courses can be wide-ranging, covering much of the ground in those areas mentioned above, but the focus is on film analysis and film theory.

Theory is not the same as criticism. Everyone, it seems, is a film critic. Criticism only requires an opinion about a film. Film theory on the other hand is a philosophical approach to organizing, dissecting, and understanding the most intricate and minute details about film and film production. Film theorists sometimes deal with such seemingly obvious issues as: What is a camera? What is a film? How is film perceived? These issues are dealt with in excruciating depth in a fundamentally philosophical and scholarly manner.

Film theorist J. Dudley Andrew in *The Major Film Theories* (1976) states that film theories are concerned with either "Raw material, methods and techniques, forms and shapes, or purpose and value." This means film theorists focus on everything about a film, from the physical materials and equipment to its value in society. Theories about film often focus on the nature of the medium, principles of aesthetics, how the form of a film can impart knowledge to the viewer, ideological (social and political) concepts of films, and the nature of reality and truth as related to and conceived of by the cinema.

As you can see, the study of film can encompass a wide, rich variety of exciting disciplines offering a wealth of ideas. Film study can be practical, it can help you to write better, to be more observant, to become more aware of the tricks that visual artists use to influence you (particularly advertisers, but filmmakers too), it can help you develop a broader vocabulary, and can introduce you to fresh ideas.

Also, if you are so motivated, there are many jobs available in the world of film and video production—many more than just in Hollywood. Businesses, TV stations, art galleries, schools, advertising agencies, and multimedia and production houses all need people who are knowledgeable about the cinema and the creation, use and presentation of visual imagery.

But film study is valuable even outside of these obvious connections. People who succeed in any field are likely to be those with creative, artistic ideas, who have a broad-based liberal arts education. Knowing about culture, the arts, communication, and the humanities will make you a better and wiser conversationalist and a more interesting and creative worker.

Film study is valuable on a personal and social level, too. These courses can enhance your enjoyment and understanding of the visual arts, make you a more knowledgeable consumer, and a more interesting person. Having more and better ideas about art, culture, society, history, literature, and communication can make you a better citizen and can enrich your personal development.

There is a world of amazement and awe ahead of you in the wonderful world of film. Oh, and it's great fun too!

Chapter Two

BECOMING A CRITICAL VIEWER
Tips for Viewing Films

"Beauty in things exists in the mind which contemplates them."
— David Hume

"Film is the art of seeing."
— Wim Wenders

eople *watch* movies. People *look* at films. But watching and looking are passive words that do not necessarily imply seeing and perceiving, which are more active, engaging activities. One can look at something but not really see it. One can watch a movie but not cognitively engage it, evaluate it, consider its meanings, its values, its ideology. How should one look at art?

When first encountering a Picasso abstract painting, a naïve viewer is typically confused, disoriented, and full of doubts; in fact, is likely to turn away in displeasure and bewilderment. This is not a fun, interesting, or informative experience. When one looks at a new, uniquely designed building, it may seem out of place, unfamiliar, and therefore ugly. When we experience art or design that we know little about, it is common to turn away or to reject it. But as one comes to know more about art and the intentions of artists, these experiences can be stimulating and arresting.

It is one thing to watch a movie and it is quite a different thing to be fully aware of a movie and its techniques and effects. It is one thing to be immersed in an experience and quite another thing to be fully aware of the experience, aware of our reaction to it, and thinking about it while engaged in it. To be involved in something, to be lost in the thing, is an entirely different phenomenal experience than to be engaged, hyper-conscious, contemplative, introspective, and thinking about the experience. It's the difference between being mentally on the inside versus being an outside observer.

To look at something is not at all the same thing as being atten-
tive of what that something is and how and why it is affecting you. To
read, to listen, and to look can be either experiences at a simple sensing
level of consciousness, or they can be experiences at a higher, meta-
conscious level. That is, you can read a story or listen to a piece of
music or look at a film in two completely different ways. The first, the
most common, is to be seduced into the experience without critically
observing and evaluating what is happening. The second is to become
a kind of outsider looking in. To see and think about a movie rather than
to watch it and get lost in it—this is critical viewing.

In order to understand and to appreciate film, it is necessary to
be a critical viewer. This is a new and different kind of mental experience than you are used to when watching movies, TV, video, or other
visual images. Critical viewing requires a different kind of attentive-
ness, awareness, and cognitive, mental thinking. You need to look and
think differently.

To become a critical viewer, one should first learn about film
techniques and film form. Critical viewing requires knowing something about how films are made, the structure of a film, the techniques,
the vocabulary, and the relationships between film and other aspects of
literature, the arts, and life's experiences. One should learn about the
history of film, the categories and types of films, the nature of a shot,
cinematography, editing, and so on. This knowledge will help you better understand the cinema, and will make you less likely to be manipulated, exploited, or seduced by visual images.

Second, learn to look at the screen differently. Critical viewers are not only wise viewers, they are also hyper-conscious viewers
who look at the screen in a different way than a normal viewer, and who
constantly and persistently engage in cognitive acts such as attention,
evaluation, and comparison while watching.

Put yourself mentally behind the camera. Imagine that you are
controlling the camera. When you look at the screen, mentally place
yourself behind the camera so that the screen is an object, like a painted canvas, that you are looking at. Try not to be engrossed only in the
story, the action and the images. Try to stay mentally separate from the
diegesis, the life and events depicted on the screen. Try to see the film
as the cinematographer sees it. Look *at* the film rather than through it,
and keep your mind always contemplative and observant rather than
lost within the story or action of the film.

Next, think about the filmmakers—their intentions, decisions,
and techniques. As you watch things unfold on the screen, ask yourself
what the director is doing and why. What is happening on the screen

right now? What precisely is happening? Why are the actors doing what they are doing? What is the composition of the shot, and how is it lit? Why did the director or the editor choose that particular shot in that particular way? What alternatives are possible, and which would have been better? Notice the transitions between shots, pay attention to the composition, the movement of the camera, the music and other sounds, and the use of computers and other special effects.

Ask yourself questions. What is going on in this scene—what *exactly* is going on in this scene? Where is the camera? Is it stationary or moving? Is it on a dolly, a crane, or is it hand-held? Is this a set or a location shot? Are there special effects being used to create illusions? Is the film manipulative or is it honest? What is the film saying beneath the story—are there subtexts, product placements, moral messages, political attitudes being expressed, social concepts and assumptions interwoven into the plot, are there stereotypes of certain groups being represented?

What messages or meanings are being conveyed by the shot and the sounds? How does the shot help to enhance or develop the story, the plot, and the characters, and how does the shot give information to the audience? Is this shot manipulative, exploitative, or stereotypical? Does it have integrity? Is it honest or is it propaganda, is it exploiting some group or person, is it true to the whole film, is it interesting or provocative, is it thought provoking, is it artistic or is it clichéd, is it redundant or repetitive, or is it fresh and insightful?

Keep thinking, keep looking, don't be seduced into letting down your guard. When you look at art, you don't need to be just an uninvolved observer pulled into the object. You can be a critical viewer. You can wonder about the art's style, its form, its messages and meanings, its integrity, its nature, and you can evaluate it.

A critical viewer has many advantages over a non-critical viewer, including being better protected from manipulation and exploitation. Critical viewers can enjoy art more and at a higher level because they have the vocabulary, insight, knowledge, and viewing skills to enhance the experience.

Chapter Three

ANALYZING FILMS
Theories, Themes, & Styles

"Every man's work, whether it be literature or music or pictures or architecture or anything else, is always a portrait of himself."
— *Samuel Butler*

Perhaps it's true that every work of art is essentially a portrait, a glimpse of the person who created it. But it is also fundamentally true that the observer's perception or interpretation of a work of art is in some sense a portrait, a glimpse of that observer. When we analyze films, when we talk about the movies, in essence we are talking about ourselves—our world, our ideas, our values, beliefs, and perceptions—the whole bit. Just as the great philosopher Ludwig Wittgenstein wrote, "The world is everything that is the case," so too we can say that a film is everything that we have to think or say about it.

Context

A film can be analyzed on many different levels, at times simultaneously. We can talk about techniques, such as editing, framing, camera angles, and the like, or we can focus on the messages and meanings, the values and purposes of the film, or we can talk about the plot, the characters, the physical locale and the sets, or we can talk about our reactions to the film, our emotions, our thoughts and memories that were stirred, or we can analyze a film's various subtexts and our theoretical opinions about what it all means. There is no right or wrong, no rules for what can or cannot be thought, felt, or said about a film. But, be careful, because this freedom to analyze a film in any possible way means that the best analysis will be judged by its honesty, its integrity, and its ability to ring true in light of the film's reality. A good analysis is one that touches the truth.

Just as a good analysis of any art—painting, music, dance, theater, poetry, and so on—will resonate with integrity, will be honest and true to the spirit and reality of the art and the audience, so too a good film analysis should leave us aware of its substance, and should inspire us to think new, more significant and enlightened ideas about the film and about life. A good film analysis can focus on any of the numerous variables involved in the art, but the analysis must ring true, it must have integrity and insight, it must be honest with respect to the artistry, meanings, and connotations of the film.

For example, it is easy to find sexism in most films today. Men are often portrayed as macho, aggressive loners while women often are given roles that emphasize nurturance, support, and weakness. Slasher movies are particularly offensive, but nearly all Hollywood films include easily identified sexist stereotypes. However, sometimes the sexism is a parody or a satire that has an ironic, social-commentary aspect that makes it legitimate, rather than a stereotypical, sophomoric exploitation. The films of Robert Altman often fit this concept. They are likely to be skewers of society, parodies of our foibles that poke fun at us and perhaps reveal some truths.

Another example is the use of violence in films. What is the message associated with the violence? Oliver Stone claims that his film *Natural Born Killers* (1994) is a parody and a warning to society that we have turned violent people into celebrities. He argues that his film is a profound and important indictment of society and its love affair with violence. Many critics and viewers, however, disagree with Stone and argue that his film is one more glorification of violence, regardless of what was the director's intent. They say that he is hypocritical and that his film is a cynical, manipulative use of violence to sell tickets; that it is not a proper and respectable social commentary. They say the evidence is that more than a dozen copycat murders occurred after viewing the film. Who's right?

Mike Leigh's film *Naked* (1994) also includes a great deal of violence, yet the context does not seem one of glorification, but rather more a dreary, realistic slice of an outcast's social life. Are there people among us who have become so desensitized to human suffering, so lacking in conscience, with such a sudden propensity to be violent at the slightest whim that this film provides an important social document of

Godard's New Wave film
Breathless (1959)

that issue? Or is *Naked* another example of gratuitous violence on the screen? A good analysis of these films must make these distinctions and be honest in appraisal and understanding of each film's merits as a work of art.

Theories

Film is a visual medium and hence uses **iconography**, visual images to convey messages. Sometimes these messages are apparent, as when we see an angry person look at a knife. Other times the images are more subtle and subconscious. One theoretical way to look at iconography, the meanings of the images presented by a film, is the theory known as **semiology** or **semiotics** (the study of signs). Semiology attempts to understand what meanings are conveyed by certain kinds of imagery. What do we think or feel when we see a flower? What is the meaning of a tree, a river, a rainstorm, a human eye, the back of a neck, or a dinner table? Are there universal messages conveyed by these images? Some critics use semiotic theory to analyze films. They are looking for the signs and symbols in the film's iconography that will cause the audience to think or feel a certain way.

Another theoretical approach to analyzing films is **auteur theory**. The term auteur is French for "author." Just as the author of a book exhibits a certain style of writing, similarly various directors have developed recognizable, signature styles of filmmaking that we can study and refer to when critiquing other films. Alfred Hitchcock is probably the best known example. His suspense films are so stylized that critics will often compare new films to his, often using the term "Hitchcockian" to refer to a film that uses many of the techniques and forms that were used by the great master.

Some films break narrative rules in the film's structure in a manner similar to the films of Jean-Luc Godard, another important film auteur. John Boorman quipped about Godard: "He is wonderfully subversive and wickedly funny. Half of what he says, I'm sure, is designed to mislead younger filmmakers." Because his films often are elliptical, manipulating chronology and linear sequences, Godard was asked if he thought films should have a beginning, a middle, and an end. He replied, "Certainly, but not necessarily in that order."

Not all directors can or should be thought of as authors, however. Many films have more the look of a particular studio's work rather than that of an individual. Also, renowned director John Ford said, "It is wrong to liken a director to an author. He is more like an architect." Still, an analysis of a film might rightly and helpfully describe it by comparing and contrasting it to the works of various film auteurs whose works have an identifiable style and motifs.

Themes

Film analysis often refers to political or ideological ideas. The works of Jean-Luc Godard and Lina Wertmuller are full of political references, often leaning toward the radical and confrontational. On the other hand, the vast majority of Hollywood films portray a conservative, moralistic message about politics. The most common theme is about justice and revenge—the idea of an eye for an eye. Most movies don't even bother to mention other possible reactions to conflict—the only reaction shown, or even considered, is revenge through violence. It's no wonder that in our culture people have such difficulty thinking of peaceful ways to deal with violence and conflict—within families, as well as within the broader society.

Similarly, it is rare to find a film that takes an openly anti-capitalistic stance, such as Michael Moore's *Roger and Me* (1989). More often, our form of government, our justice and economic systems, and other status quo institutional and social systems are inherently ingrained into and supported by Hollywood movies. There is a very limited range of freedom of speech in the movie industry. Movie studios don't want to upset the viewers, hence their movies reflect majority views and provide only happy endings. If film is an art, then why do movie studios have test showings to gauge audience response and change their films accordingly?

Sex and violence are common elements in nearly all Hollywood movies, and the theme is spreading worldwide. But moralists show much more concern for portrayal of the former, that is sex, than for the latter, violence. For some odd and unfortunate reason, violence is a widely accepted subject for entertainment. When it comes to rating the movies, sex is considered much worse for children than is violence. Actor Jack Nicholson correctly observed, "If you suck a tit, you're an X—cut it off with a sword, you're a GP."

Notorious (1946)

For many years there was a Hollywood Production Code that regulated what could and could not be included in movies. Many foreign and independent films were banned in the U.S. because they did not conform to the Code. One of the prohibitions was that a kiss could not be held for very long. Alfred Hitchcock got around this rule in *Notorious* (1946) by having Ingrid Bergman start and stop kissing Cary Grant many times in one scene. Similarly, the Code demanded that an immoral person be punished at the end of the film, thereby sanctifying the revenge motivation that is the hallmark of most Hollywood films today.

Styles

When analyzing a film, a good place to begin is to think about the difference between form and content. For instance, a painting of a tree (the content) can be done in many different styles (the form). Similarly, novels about the same event, say the Civil War, can be written in entirely different styles. When looking at a film, think about the content as one element and the form or style of presentation as another. For example, a science fiction movie can be done in a very realistic style, such as Stanley Kubrick's *2001: A Space Odyssey* (1968), which today looks much more realistic and accurate than much more recent films. A completely different form can be found in Fritz Lang's classic *Metropolis* (1926), which is an expressionistic film that does not try to look like reality, but instead attempts to be evocative, stylized, and artistic.

The computer HAL reads lips in
2001: A Space Odyssey

It is interesting to think about how the content and the form of a film fit together or complement each other. The Danish film *The Celebration* (1998), for example, was shot with a hand-held digital 8mm camera, giving the film a grainy, jumpy look. This nicely complements the story about some very upsetting circumstances at a family's birthday party. In *Persona* (1966), at the point during which a woman experiences a split or breakdown in her personality, the film literally tears and the form of the film suddenly changes from a calm, introspective style to an abrupt, confusing, nearly **non-narrative** form.

The Robot's face in *Metropolis,* an expressionist film

Most modern Hollywood movies, unfortunately, have adopted a formulaic style entirely irrespective of the content of the movie. Very often you will find rapid cutting and swirling cameras even in movies that attempt to present content that is serious, deliberative, or moving. On the contrary, Michelangelo Antonioni's *L'Avventura* (1960) uses long shots of nearly barren landscapes to indicate loneliness and alienation. When the film was first shown at the Cannes Film Festival the audience became so restless and frustrated with the film's form that they yelled, "Cut, cut" at the screen!

The film image signals a nervous breakdown in *Persona*

The degree to which a work of art resembles the world as we actually see it is called **verisimilitude**. A realistic film is high in verisimilitude, while abstract shapes, incongruous colors, distortions, and machine-made designs are low in verisimilitude. Some artists believe that art should be as realistic as possible. Realist painters went even further and argued that art should not only replicate what the world looks like (be high in verisimilitude) but that art also should deal only with subjects that are ordinary and common in our experience.

Other artists feel that reality is well suited to the real world and that art should show us what otherwise can't be seen. Famed Danish director Carl Dreyer wrote, "We have to wrench the film out of the embrace of naturalism. We have to tell ourselves it is a waste of time to copy reality. We must use the camera to create a new language of style, a new artistic form."

Some of these artists even challenge the idea that art can show reality. Fellini said, "What's the use of being 'objective' in film? I don't think it's physically possible."

Photocopy Cha Cha

An oft-told story recounts how a man said he didn't like abstract art because it didn't look real. He was asked by an abstract artist what looked real to him. The man responded by showing the artist a photograph of his wife. The artist looked at it and replied that she was pretty, but very small!

Formalism is the idea that art should be stylized and imaginative in such a way as to express the artist's visions and ideas. Formalism de-emphasizes the content (the subject or the story) and instead focuses on presentation and manipulation of the medium— the form.

For example, the short film *Photocopy Cha Cha* (1991) includes images made by or suggested by a photocopy machine—but the images often are distorted and manipulated. The high-tech concept is rendered more poetic and organic by filmmaker Chel White's sensibility and stylization.

Most films have some degree of realism and some formalism. But a few are in the extreme. The experimental film *Symphonie Diagonale* (1924) consists solely of the appearance and disappearance of lines in various patterns and arrays. This is a good example of the attempt of a formalist (in this case the artist Viking Eggeling) to analyze subjects abstractly, to try to squeeze out some truth about aesthetics, design, and relationships, rather than to merely represent a real, commonplace subject.

An abstract image from
Symphony Diagonale

Intentions

One final point to consider when analyzing the cinema is its intention or purpose. In this regard, it may be helpful to distinguish between movies and films. The term "movie" is sometimes used to refer to cinematic productions that are made purely for entertainment in order to make money. A movie does not aspire to art, it aspires to the bottom line. Movies are not made by artists, they are made by businessmen. Profit is the goal.

The term "film," on the other hand, is often used to indicate a cinematic work that has some non-monetary goal, some artistic purpose—such as expression, communication, or aesthetic value. A film atttempts to be more than mere entertainment or a product for profit. A film aims at something more, has a different purpose, such as expression of a political or social view, an artistic idea to explore or to communicate, a statement about philosophy, morality, or aesthetics, or the expression of an artist's vision.

Not all film critics and scholars make this distinction (for example, famous film critic Pauline Kael preferred the term "movie" in all cases), but it is often a useful way to think about a film—to include in your analysis some thoughts about the filmmaker's goals and purposes, and whether or not a film satisfies a desire for amusement and diversion, or whether it strives for or reaches some higher artistic level. Often the distinction becomes clear long after viewing a film when you contemplate what you remember, how it affected you, and what imprint the film's ideas and meanings had on you and others.

Of course, analyzing films depends largely on having knowledge of the history of the medium, on its modes of production, and the structure and grammar of film form. Accordingly, the next section will deal with these issues.

PART TWO

Understanding

Film

he second part of this book deals with the nature and structure of films. The intention is to help the reader master some of the knowledge required for a proper and informed discussion and evaluation of the art and craft of the cinema. Chapter Four presents a brief history of the cinema covering the high points of the past one hundred years and listing the films and filmmakers that were the most influential and today are referred to the most often. Mastering the history of film will help the reader understand not only the cinema's development as an art and as an industry, but will also unveil the styles, genres, and classic works that a modern film analysis will invariable refer to for purposes of comparison and contrast.

The next chapter of this part, "What is Film?" details important vocabulary and terminology about the physical nature of film and the process of making and exhibiting movies. Just as with all disciplines, film study has its own distinctive vocabulary and way of approaching its subject. This information will help the reader to better communicate about film and will subsequently make the reader a better evaluator of film. Included in Chapter Five is information about the raw material of film, film production, and the structure of film—that is, a description of film terminology and techniques regarding the fundamental ingredient of any film, the shot. This chapter explains different kinds of shots and how shots are put together, that is, the different means of making transitions from shot to shot. Since films are fundamentally made of shots (the shot is the *cell* of a film), an understanding of how and why shots work is basic to understanding and talking about films.

The final chapter of Part Two, "Cognition and Meaning," discusses important ideas about evaluating films and other arts with regard to the meanings that they convey. It is argued that this is the most salient criterion in appraising art and is the essential ingredient in our understanding of how art relates to us, how it complements and fulfills our lives. A work of art is successful to the degree that it conveys some fundamental truths about the human condition, our emotions, our experiences, our beliefs, and our ideas. To the extent that a film can provide an honest, daring, and illuminating truth, it will be judged as a successful work of art.

While this middle section of this book is concerned with the understanding of film, it is essentially a preparation for the third part, the appraisal of film as an art form. But in order to make judgments about film as art it is first necessary to understand what film is, its history, its structure, its nature, and more significantly, to understand the importance of meaning in the interpretation and evaluation of the arts.

Chapter Four

A BRIEF HISTORY OF FILM
A Century of Cinema

"If there's a way of saying I love you without saying it—that's film."
— Buster Keaton

*T*he cinema is a modern invention that just recently celebrated its one-hundredth birthday. In the mid to late nineteenth century people enjoyed toys and spinning devices and projection machines that gave the illusion of movement—such as a series of sequential pictures flashed quickly before the eyes, or the **Kinetoscope**, a large box holding a short spool of film that a single person could view, or the **magic lantern** (an early form of a slide projector), or puppet and shadow shows—but there were no cinema theaters until nearly 1900. So, the cinema is truly a twentieth century phenomenon.

Beginnings

By the 1890s inventors around the world, including those working for Thomas Edison, were developing machines for recording and projecting motion pictures. The first time that movies were projected on a screen for a paying audience was in Paris, France on December 28, 1895. The few short films that were shown had been made by brothers Auguste and Louis Lumière (coincidentally, their name means "light") who owned a photographic equipment company in Lyons, France. They invented a camera (the Cinematographe) that could record and also project images at a very fast rate, giving the illusion of movement. The Cinematographe held a reel of film that lasted less than a minute. The Lumières did no editing, the movies they showed were uninterrupted shots lasting 15 to 20 seconds. They attached their camera to a tripod and recorded real, everyday events.

A Lumière brothers' actualité:
Arrival of a Train

Therefore, the Lumière brothers are known as the founders of Realism in the cinema. The first film they exhibited showed workers leaving their factory. They also showed an actualité, as their films are known, of a train arriving at a station, a short film that has become famous as ushering-in the age of movies.

In the Lumières' audience was a French magician named Georges Méliès who was so intrigued by this new technology that he decided to use it in his theater. Méliès built his own camera, and later his own recording studio. He made the first staged fantasy films and is therefore known as the founder of fantastic or fictional films. Méliès' best-known film is *A Trip to the Moon* (1902), a sci-fi adventure that featured a rocket hitting the moon. The moon was depicted with a human face, that of Méliès himself. Méliès also was the first to use special camera tricks to create illusions or special effects on film, such as superimposition. The best known of his camera tricks is the "pop-up" or stop motion shot. The camera is stopped, objects are moved around, and the camera starts up again. The result is an unexpected, humorous change in the scene, such as a hat suddenly appearing on a man's head.

A Trip to the Moon (1902)

Early Narrative Films

In the United States, Edwin Porter made a Western titled *The Great Train Robbery* (1903) in which he used innovative editing techniques that became conventional in later films and helped establish the basic principles of continuity editing (shots put together to tell a continuous story). For example, his film cuts back and forth between two different events, a method known as **parallel editing** or cross-cutting.

The Babylon set in *Intolerance*

D. (David) W. (Wark) Griffith was the major U.S. filmmaker early in the twentieth century and today is often referred to as the father of the narrative film and classical editing techniques. Griffith's film *The Birth of a Nation* (1915) is a large-scale depiction of the Civil War and exemplifies the state of the art in filmmaking for its time. Unfortunately, the film represented racist ideas and the widespread criticism of his film bothered Griffith very much. In an attempt to exonerate himself he made *Intolerance* (1916), an expensive and ambitious film that used **thematic montage** (a technique in which several different storylines are interwoven) as well as very large sets, including the famous Babylon set, perhaps the largest set ever built for a film.

Comedy movies were very popular in the early years of filmmaking and one of the greatest comedians and filmmakers was Charles (Charlie) Chaplin who became the first worldwide movie star. Chaplin's films were personal, humanistic, heart-felt, often commented on social injustice, and were full of romanticism and slapstick comedy. *The Gold Rush* (1925), *City Lights* (1931), and *Modern Times* (1936)

Charlie Chaplin in *Modern Times*

are often rated as his best efforts. Another comic filmmaker who deserves mention is Buster Keaton, whose sad, expressive face and daredevil antics are unparalleled to this day. His droll romps reached perfection in *Our Hospitality* (1923), *Sherlock Jr.* (1924), and *Steamboat Bill Jr.* (1928).

Buster Keaton

Dr. Caligari introduces his somnambulist to Jane

Early Artists

D. W. Griffith's many films typify the approach taken by U.S. filmmakers, that of fictional storytelling and conventional narrative editing. Meanwhile, in Germany a new style of films was emerging known as **Expressionism**. Artists made films that looked unreal, extreme, angular, and stylized. The sets were imaginary, the actors were overly dramatic, and the stories were wild. Their idea was that film, just as other arts, should express the inner visions and imaginings of the artist, rather than merely represent everyday life.

The Cabinet of Dr. Caligari (1919) is often cited as the first and best example of German Expressionism. Its story concerns a series of murders committed by a hypnotized zombie controlled by a mad doctor. Renowned filmmaker Fritz Lang contributed the visionary, futuristic film *Metropolis* (1926) which imagines the year 2000. Lang made many important films including his first sound film, *M* (1931), the tale of a child murderer. Perhaps the best of the early German directors, F. W. Murnau made the expressionistic films *Nosferatu* (1922), the first vampire film, and *Faust* (1926), the tale of a man who sells his soul to the devil. Murnau experimented with camera movements in *The Last Laugh* (1924) and went to

Hollywood where he made the very beautiful *Sunrise* (1927).

Several other 1920-30s German directors went to Hollywood where they enjoyed great success. Good examples are Josef von Sternberg whose film *The Blue Angel* (1930) starring Marlene Dietrich was made in both German and English, and Ernst Lubitsch who often made romantic comedies such as *Ninotchka* (1939) and *The Shop Around the Corner* (1940), which Nora Ephron re-made as *You've Got Mail* in 1998.

Metropolis (1926)

German Expressionism inspired Hollywood in the 1930s to make a series of horror and gothic films such as *Frankenstein* (1931), *Dracula* (1931), and *Wuthering Heights* (1939). Today many films use Expressionism to some extent and a few filmmakers emphasize an expressionistic style. Examples include Tim Burton (*Batman*, 1989) and the French team of Jean-Pierre Jeunet and Marc Caro (*Delicatessen*, 1991 and *The City of Lost Children*, 1995).

Sunrise (1927)

In France, the leading early filmmaker was Abel Gance whose *Napoleon* (1927) used three projectors to create a wide-screen effect, and *J'Accuse* (1919 and 1938) included filmed footage of World War I in a powerful anti-war tale. Later, Jean Renoir, son of the famous French painter Pierre-Auguste Renoir,

Jean Renoir in *Rules of the Game*

became the leading French filmmaker and created the masterpieces *Grand Illusion* (1937) and *Rules of the Game* (1939). Renoir's films exude grace, fluidity, complexity, and a humane attitude. Renoir was a master of **mise-en-scene**, the choreographing and arranging of elements within the film frame.

Variations

Not all early filmmakers were interested in fictional story-telling. Led by Robert Flaherty, a new style of film called a **documentary** evolved. The idea was to show something real, but to make it

interesting as well as informative, and to give it a point of view—the filmmaker shows reality in such a way that it expresses an opinion. British film scholar John Grierson coined the term documentary and defined it as "the creative treatment of actuality." Flaherty's *Nanook of the North* (1922), the story of an Inuit (Canadian Eskimo) man and his family surviving the barren terrain near Hudson Bay, is often referred to as the granddaddy of documentary films.

Some filmmakers wanted to explore the outer boundaries, the possibilities of film. This category is known as experimental or **avant-garde** (out in front) films and is often populated by creative artists interested in film

Nanook of the North
(1922)

for the sake of art rather than for commercial success. Early experimenters included Hans Richter, Viking Eggeling, Man Ray, Marcel Duchamp, and Fernand Leger. Their films are short, abstract, artistic, imaginative, and thought provoking. For example, *Ballet Mecanique* (1924) by Leger, *Ghosts Before Breakfast* (1928) by Richter, and *Symphonie Diagonale* (1924) by Eggeling use disjointed and **non-narrative** (does not tell a story) elements.

Jean Cocteau's creativity shows in
The Blood of a Poet

One of the most creative artists in history was Frenchman Jean Cocteau whose films had a poetic and innovative visual style, such as *The Blood of a Poet* (1930), *Beauty and the Beast* (1946), and *Orpheus* (1950). Another film artist, Luis Buñuel, born in Spain, catapulted onto the filmmaking scene with *Un Chien Andalou* (1929) made in collaboration with artist Salvador Dali. Their film was made according to the principles of **Surrealism**, an art move-

A surrealistic image from
Un Chien Andalou

ment based on the concept of attempting to reveal the unconscious mind. Surrealists put their dreams into their art. Buñuel made numerous films in which he satirized and mocked religious, political, and social conventions. His best work includes *L'Age D'Or* (1930), *Viridiana* (1962), *The Exterminating Angel* (1967), and *The Phantom of Liberty* (1974).

Innovations

During the 1920s, Russian filmmaking was second to none, perhaps because the people involved were so intelligent and driven. The Russians were fascinated by the work of Griffith and Flaherty, but Russian film scholars probably led the world in developing film theories and ideas at that time in history. Sergei Eisenstein emerged as the most successful of the group and his theories about editing influenced the world.

The best known and most studied example is the Odessa steps sequence from the film *Battleship Potemkin* (1925). Eisenstein pieced together many small bits of film in a certain prescribed order according to his editing theory. The result was a rapid succession of images depicting the Czar's soldiers killing people on a long stairway in the city of Odessa. This

Part of the Odessa steps montage

sequence became the most studied piece of film in history. The technique is known as **montage**, a French term meaning "assembly," and Eisenstein's work created a revolution in the way films were edited.

This is one of the key ingredients of any film and filmmakers must ask themselves how much and to what extent and what kind of montage they should use.

Another influential Russian filmmaker was Dziga Vertov (Denis Kaufman's made-up name, which means Rrruzz Spinning Top!) who taught that a camera was an eye on the world and that films should show us the essence of our surroundings. He called this approach **Kino Pravda** (cinema truth) and his film *The Man with the Movie Camera* (1929) became a sensation. Vertov included special effects, camera tricks, and fast editing, all of which made his films stand out from the crowd.

French filmmakers adopted this eye on the world concept and called it **cinema vérité** (cinema truth) and in the U.S. it is sometimes called direct cinema. In this method, films are made by recording everyday events with no actors, no script, no sets, and no directions—the world is captured on film without any tinkering. Today there is no one better known for this approach than Frederick Wiseman, whose films include *Titicut Follies* (1967), a candid and harrowing look inside a mental health facility (the film was banned for years!), and *High School* (1969).

Nonfiction films are well represented by the work of D. A. Pennebaker whose films include the Bob Dylan concert movie, *Don't Look Back* (1967) and *Monterey Pop* (1968). Some films blurred the line between fiction and documentary, such as the rule-breaking first movie starring the Beatles, *A Hard Day's Night* (1964), directed by Richard Lester. Also, today the hybrid or **docudrama** (a fictional account based on a true event), such as *Heavenly Creatures* (New Zealand, 1994), is very common and popular.

The Main Stream

Many experts believe that films were best when they were silent, that the use of sound detracted from the importance of the visual image. But once sound-films were developed in the late 1920s, audiences would not go to the silents anymore, they demanded talkies. With rare exceptions, all films made after 1929 used sound. *The Jazz Singer* (1927) is recognized as the first film with synchronized sound, although nonsynch sound was used in earlier films.

Films were full of sound and color by 1939, a year rich with productions such as *Gone With the Wind* and *The Wizard of Oz*. Major Hollywood directors were emerging during the 1930s and 1940s such as

John Ford who made beautiful black and white morality tales, typically Westerns starring John Wayne. *Stagecoach* (1939) and *The Grapes of Wrath* (1940) are two of his best efforts. Frank Capra was another important director of that period who specialized in warm-hearted, down-to-earth, sentimental stories about human struggles. *It Happened One Night* (1934), *Mr. Deeds Goes to Town* (1936), *Mr. Smith Goes to Washington* (1939), *Meet John Doe* (1941), and *It's a Wonderful Life* (1946) are good examples of his movies. Preston Sturges made witty, socially-conscious films such as *Sullivan's Travels* (1941), Michael Curtiz was a prolific studio pro who directed the immensely popular *Casablanca* (1942), and John Huston contributed *The Maltese Falcon* (1941), *Treasure of the Sierra Madre* (1948), and *The African Queen* (1951).

Hollywood in the 1930s and 1940s was controlled by the major studios and the movies they produced were formulaic, following certain genre styles. For example, screwball comedies were common as well as musicals, horror films, and epics.

Changes Due

By the 1940s virtually all films followed the same format and were ready for a change. One of the most important new developments came from Italy where citizens were suffering from the effects of World War II. In response, filmmakers wanted to express the lives of everyday people and thus developed a film style known as Italian **Neorealism**. Using non-professional actors, on-location filming, simple cinematography, limited editing, no special effects, and an emphasis on common people with everyday concerns, these films were immensely moving, and seemed almost like documentaries or even cinema vérité. Roberto Rossellini's *Open City* (1945) is often cited as one of the first and most influential of the neorealist films, and Vittorio De Sica's *The Bicycle Thief* (1948) is typically rated as the most profound and representative of that style.

Non-professional actors in
The Bicycle Thief

Italy later provided the film world with two of its most distinguished directors. Federico Fellini began working on neorealist films

The neo-noir film, *Blade Runner*

but expanded his **oeuvre** (total body of work) to include a rich assortment of masterpieces including *La Strada* (1954), *La Dolce Vita* (1960), *8 1/2* (1963), and *Amarcord* (1974). The other Italian filmmaking legend is Michelangelo Antonioni, whose films such as *L'Avventura* (1960) and *The Eclipse* (1962) are slow, hypnotic, existential commentaries on loneliness, relationships, and alienation in modern society.

In the United States another style was emerging in the 1940s that French film scholars dubbed **film noir** (black cinema). These films looked dark because of the way that scenes were lit—heavy with shadows—and they also portrayed dark themes, such as crime, deception, and the evil side of people. Always there was a *femme fatale*, a beautiful woman who led men astray and ultimately proved to be cunning and deceitful. Billy Wilder's *Double Indemnity* (1944) and *Sunset Boulevard* (1950) are classic examples of film noir. Nearly a hundred such films were made in the 1940s-50s, and even today many films are influenced by that style, films known as neo-noir, such as *Body Heat* (1981), *Blade Runner* (1982), and *L. A. Confidential* (1997).

Some filmmakers resurrected the **avant-garde** film, a style that gained a good deal of popularity beginning in 1943 with a film by Maya Deren titled *Meshes of the Afternoon*. The film is a personal, poetic piece of art that inspired many other filmmakers and viewers.

Maya Deren in her avant-garde film
Meshes of the Afternoon

The interest in avant-garde film continued into the 1960s and included the work of actor John Cassavetes whose films, such as *Shadows* (1960), were fresh, startling, improvisational gems. Stanley Brakhage (e.g., *Dog Star Man*, 1964) has contributed hundreds of films, and continues to make personal, often poetic experimentations in form and cinematography, many in which he scratches or paints on the filmstock itself.

Orson Welles in *Touch of Evil*

Perhaps the greatest cinematic achievement came from theatrical genius Orson Welles whose first film, *Citizen Kane* (1941), is often hailed as the greatest and most influential American film ever made. Welles used rich cinematography, dense mise-en-scene, and clever film techniques to create a lavish story about the American dream that was based on real-life newspaperman William Randolph Hearst. Orson Welles went on to create many more fascinating films including the highly praised film noir *Touch of Evil* (1958).

The Peak of Film Art

The 1950s were a time of problems and opportunities. First there was the Cold War with the Soviet Union and the fear of Communism that led to intense paranoia, censorship, and witch hunts. Many great artists in the film industry were blacklisted by the government and unable to find work in movies. Some became ghostwriters in order to disguise their identity, as described in *The Front* (1976). The documentary *Point of Order!* (1964) offers an unsettling look at the McCarthy hearings.

A second development was that television became a fixture in many homes in the 1950s and the cinema felt threatened. One response was to change the proportions of the screen—thus, the advent of widescreen movies that continues to this day.

Films before 1950 had the same frame proportion as a TV screen, about one third wider than they are high. Modern films are nearly two times wider than they are high, and sometimes even wider. This change in **aspect ratio** created many new problems and opportunities for filmmakers. *Lawrence of Arabia* (1962) by David Lean of Great

Britain is a good example of a film that took advantage of the wide-screen format.

The 1950s and 1960s were an exciting time of many changes in the cinema. Besides widescreen, new color systems were developed that made films more vibrant and more interesting than TV and some studios produced movies that were perceived in 3-D when viewed with special glasses. Also during this period, film was reaching a peak in artistic expression.

Wild Strawberries stars early Swedish director Victor Sjöström

In Sweden, film director Ingmar Bergman was creating a place in history for his style of artistic and philosophical cinema. Perhaps no one has equaled his excellence in film output. Such films as *The Seventh Seal* (1957), *Wild Strawberries* (1957), *Persona* (1966), and *Cries and Whispers* (1972) are profound, timeless masterpieces of art that earned Bergman the Cannes Film Festival award as greatest film director in history.

Another great director who reached his peak in the 1950s was Alfred Hitchcock, who became known as the master of suspense. His films are chilling, mysterious, thoughtful, regularly romantic, and feature familiar and beloved movie stars such as Jimmy Stewart, Cary Grant, and Grace Kelly. Hitchcock's best films include *Rear Window* (1954), *Vertigo* (1958), *North By Northwest* (1959), and *Psycho* (1960).

The American Stanley Kubrick became disenchanted with the studio approach after finishing the Hollywood spectacle *Spartacus* (1960) and moved to England to independently make films according to his own ideals. His oeuvre is among cinema's greatest. *Dr. Strangelove or: How I Learned to Stop Worrying and Love the Bomb* (1964) is a biting satire about the Cold War and the atomic bomb, and *2001: A Space Odyssey* (1968) forever changed the look, sound (use of classical music), and idea (intelligent life, rather than attacking enemies) of sci-fi films.

Meanwhile, in France young thinkers were developing a new theory about the cinema and creating their own inexpensive, excitingly fresh films known for breaking film's conventional rules. This movement became known as the **French New Wave** (*Nouvelle Vague*). Many influential films were produced by this adventurous group including *Breathless* (1959), My *Life to Live* (1962), *Band of Outsiders*

(1964), and *Weekend* (1967) by Jean-Luc Godard, perhaps history's most political and intellectual filmmaker; *The 400 Blows* (1959), *Shoot the Piano Player* (1960), *Jules and Jim* (1962), and *Day for Night* (1973) by François Truffaut, one of history's most interesting and beloved filmmakers; and *Hiroshima, mon Amour* (1959) by Alain Resnais, whose films are often beautiful, complex, carefully crafted enigmas of human intelligence, especially involving memory, consciousness, and aspects of time. *Last Year at Marienbad* (1961) is a stunning example.

Jules and Jim is more about a woman's search for identity than about the title men.

Like France, Germany also experienced a new wave period that is known as *Das Neue Kino*. Led by extraordinary young directors Werner Herzog (*Aguirre: Wrath of God*, 1973 and *Fitzcarraldo*, 1982), Rainer Werner Fassbinder (*The Marriage of Maria Braun*, 1979), and Wim Wenders (*Wings of Desire*, 1987), Germany once again regained the filmmaking excellence it had exhibited in the 1920s.

Asian countries also reached high notes in film production. Akira Kurosawa of Japan stands as one of cinema's finest masters. His *The Seven Samurai* (1954) inspired numerous other films around the world. In India, Satyajit Ray's films were visually and emotionally powerful tales of humanistic social issues, particularly *The Apu Trilogy* (1956-59). In recent years a few filmmakers in Iran have resurrected the neorealist spirit with gentle, philosophical tales of everyday life. Abbas Kiarostami (*Taste of Cherry*, 1997) and Mohsen Makhmalbaf (*The Cyclist*, 1989) are among the most interesting of today's filmmakers. Similarly, China has recently had an explosion of excellent films, among them the work of Chen Kaige (*Yellow Earth*, 1984 and *Farewell My Concubine*, 1992) and his former cinematographer, Zhang Yimou (*Ju Dou*, 1989 and *Raise the Red Lantern*, 1991), both of whom use lush, vivid colors and natural landscapes in creating films concerning social and political issues in their homeland. Both the Iranian and Chinese films had censorship problems in their countries.

Eastern Europe has always produced great films and great filmmakers. Countries such as Poland, Hungary, and Czechoslovakia have always educated and encouraged cinema artists. Andrzej Wajda,

Chinese actress Gong Li in *Ju Dou*

Roman Polanski, and Krzysztof Kieslowski all hailed from Poland and made remarkable films, the best of which include (respectively) *Ashes and Diamonds* (1958), *Repulsion* (1965), and *Red* (1994).

Milos Forman of Czechoslovakia made *Loves of a Blonde* (1965) and, in Hollywood, *One Flew Over the Cuckoo's Nest* (1975) and *Amadeus* (1984). Other notable films from Eastern Europe include *Closely Watched Trains* (1966) by Jiri Menzel; *Underground* (1996) by Bosnian Emir Kusterica; *Europa Europa* (1991) by Agnieszka Holland; and *Latcho Drom* (1995), a documentary about gypsy people by Tony Gatlif.

The Present

Hollywood films have changed drastically in the last 30 years. Some notable films of the recent past include *The Graduate* (1967), *Bonnie and Clyde* (1967), *Midnight Cowboy* (1969), *Chinatown* (1974) and some of David Lynch's work, such as his experimental piece, *Eraserhead* (1977), and *The Elephant Man* (1980) and *Blue Velvet* (1986). Even most of these films, however, relied heavily on the star system, which markets actors instead of plot, style, aesthetics, or substance, to draw an audience.

But in the 1970s Hollywood made a revolutionary change by targeting the male teenage audience with huge-budget blockbusters full of special effects, action, impossible feats, and male heroics. The success of these films, with tie-ins to toys and fast food, has strangled artistic expression in modern Hollywood cinema. Many cinephiles (lovers of film) feel that the best of Hollywood is gone forever.

Great films today come from around the world. China, Iran,

Eastern Europe, Scandinavia, and South American countries are producing some of the world's most artistic cinema. Perhaps the most daring contemporary filmmakers are the group of directors from Denmark
who have created a manifesto called Dogma 95 in which they have
agreed to certain rules in making a film that will challenge the director
and the audience. Lars von Trier is among this group. His films
Zentropa (1991) and *Breaking the Waves* (1996) demonstrate a risk-taking and visionary, artistic hand. The best of Dogma 95 is *The
Celebration* (1998) by Thomas Vinterberg. Filmed in digital Hi-8 and
transferred to 35 millimeter, the film presents a unique and audacious
look, a film essentially for film experts because of its challenging and
artistic style. Some feature films today are being shot in digital format
because it is much cheaper. Soon theaters will be equipped to project
digital films and the days of celluloid projection will be over.

Today in the United States a
few contemporary directors aim at cinema art. Robert Altman continues to
make some of the most interesting
modern films, such as *Nashville* (1975)
and *The Player* (1991). Similarly, New
York filmmaker Woody Allen has created a fascinating oeuvre. Some of his
best are *Annie Hall* (1977), *Manhattan*
(1979), *Zelig* (1983), and *Hannah and
Her Sisters* (1986).

Also working in New York
(and like Woody Allen), Spike Lee
writes, directs, and stars in his films.
His best work is *Do the Right Thing*
(1989). Another New Yorker, Martin
Scorsese, a former film scholar, is a
director with a singular and meticulous
taste who is best known for his intense
films *Taxi Driver* (1976) and *Raging
Bull* (1980). Francis Ford Coppola is a
flamboyant and driven director who
achieved a good deal of success in the

Woody Allen in *Sleeper* (1973)

1970s, particularly with the lavish Vietnam War epic, *Apocalypse Now*
(1979), and the popular *Godfather* trilogy (1972, 1974, 1990).

While Hollywood since the 1970s has concentrated on films
for children and teenagers (it is said that Hollywood movies are about
children, no matter what their age, while European films are about

adults, no matter what their age) specializing in action, special effects, machismo, and slick production, independent filmmakers have provided the most interesting, provocative, and artful films.

Jim Jarmusch broke on the scene in 1984 with the masterful *Stranger Than Paradise* and has since added *Down By Law* (1986), *Mystery Train* (1989), *Night on Earth* (1991), and others. Errol Morris uses a directed documentary style in which witnesses speak to him and the camera simultaneously, as in *Mr. Death* (1999) and *The Thin Blue Line* (1988). Hal Hartley has a unique and endearing style that is intelligent, thought provoking, and heavy on dialogue. His best work includes *The Unbelievable Truth* (1989), *Trust* (1990), *Flirt* (1996), and *Henry Fool* (1998).

Many other independent filmmakers have provided thoughtful films that have aspired toward art, such as *Buffalo 66* (1998) by Vincent Gallo and *Pi* (1998) by Darren Aronofsky. However, in recent years Hollywood studios have noticed the relative excellence of independently produced films and have rushed to take advantage of them by controlling their distribution and exhibition. The result is that it is difficult today to find any truly independent films or any theaters that will exhibit avant-garde or other films that challenge the Hollywood formula. Independent films today look much like Hollywood studio productions, with slick appearance and concentration on silly plots, sex, guns, and young adults who act like children. Independent films have become a genre in their own right—simply another genre rather than an alternative.

The big-budget blockbusters of Hollywood are today influencing films around the world (for example, they easily dominate the box-office in Italy, where film was once among the world's best—how sad!) and it is becoming rare to find films that exhibit any experimentation or mature, adult themes. Those who want artistic, avant-garde, or philosophical cinema have learned to stay home or to venture out only to art houses, film societies, or museums. That is the state of the cinema today.

Are the movies dead, as proclaimed by writers Susan Sontag ("The Decay of Cinema"—see Chapter Nine) and David Thomson? In 1996 Thomson asked "Who Killed the Movies?" and answered: "Spielberg and Lucas." He added, "This medium seems to have lost its heart. Is it dead? If not, where is that stink coming from?"

We can only wonder whence cinema art will arise in the future.

Chapter Five

WHAT IS FILM?
Creating the Moving Image

"A film lives, becomes alive, because of its shadows, its spaces."
— Michael Cimino

"Most of all I miss working with Sven Nykvist, perhaps because we are both utterly captivated by the problems of light, the gentle, dangerous, dreamlike, living, dead, clear, misty, hot, violent, bare, sudden, dark, springlike, falling, straight, slanting, sensual, subdued, limited, poisonous, calming, pale light. Light."
— Ingmar Bergman

ilm is the capturing of light, the recording of light in all its dimensions. Film is the projecting of light, and the receiving and interpreting of light by the viewer. But the seemingly simple question, "What is film?" becomes very complex when we realize how many different elements and details are involved, how light is captured, projected, and ultimately perceived by a human brain. Thinking about the details of cinema makes us realize that there are at least three categories that need to be addressed regarding the question, "What is film?"

1) <u>The Equipment</u>: A large amount of physical and technical equipment, including the raw materials, is necessary for the recording, preparation, and projection of film. This includes the filmstock itself, equipment needed for shooting, a camera, lighting equipment, developing and editing machines, a projector, and more.

2) <u>The Production</u>: A film *can* be made by one person alone, but typically the production of cinema employs hundreds or thousands of people with different skills and knowledge. The various filmmaking roles include writers, producers, directors, actors, camera operators, developers, editors, and so on.

3) <u>The Structure of Film</u>: A film is made of shots. A **shot** is the lowest common denominator of a film's structure—the basic unit of a film—it is an unbroken piece of cinema. That is what films are made of—shots. Therefore, the production of a film involves planning and executing many shots, then determining the various means of transition from shot to shot, and finally editing the film by piecing together the shot sequences. So, the fundamental activity in making a movie involves taking shots and then later piecing them together.

The answer to the question, "What is film?" is thus loaded with details, complexities and ambiguities, which can lead to interesting debate that may not be at first apparent. For a deeper and more complete understanding of the cinema, here are some important points to be considered regarding the above three categories:

The Equipment

Film, that is, the physical strip before it is exposed to light, is called **filmstock**. Its base is made of a flexible plastic material called celluloid that is coated with emulsion that is sensitive to light. Color film usually has three emulsions, each sensitive to a different wavelength of light. The filmstock base was once made of nitrate, a substance that is unstable. Most films made on nitrate are no longer presentable and a good deal of time and effort is being made to transfer nitrate films to longer lasting safety base filmstock. However, film is one of the least permanent art mediums and all films deteriorate relatively quickly. This does not give the film medium much permanence; unfortunately most early films have been lost.

Filmstock has small sprocket holes regularly punched near its edges that are used to pull the film through the camera and the projector. The width of the film is known as the film **gauge** and is measured in millimeters. The smallest is 8mm wide. Educational and institutional films are usually recorded on 16mm gauge, while typical Hollywood and foreign feature films use 35mm or sometimes even

70mm gauge film. The wider the film, the more details of visual information that can be included. Therefore, some filmmakers prefer 70mm
film gauge. These films, however, are typically shot in 35mm then later
transferred to 70mm. Few movie theaters are equipped to project 70mm
gauge films, so 35mm prints are regularly distributed. For example,
Jurassic Park (1993) was released in both 35mm and 70mm.
Interestingly, the Danish film *The Celebration* (1998) was shot in digital 8mm and then transferred to 35mm, which makes for a very intriguing look.

        The strip of film is divided into frames that are rectangular in
shape, and each frame contains a still photograph. Special machines
can duplicate these frames and you will see frame enlargements printed
in film studies textbooks and other books about the cinema. The studios
also release posed photographs from the shooting of a movie and books
sometimes include those in addition to or in place of frame enlargements. It is important to distinguish between these two since the promotional photos may not appear exactly the same in the film and thereby in their details may give a misleading idea about the film's iconography and the filmmaker's style and intentions.

        Today it is common for a film to be projected onto the screen
at a rate of 24 frames per second. However, films early in this century
were often photographed and projected at between 16 and 22 frames per
second. If a film was originally recorded at 16 frames per second and
is shown on a modern projector at 24 frames per second, the action will
seem to move faster than normal and the film length will be shortened.
In contemporary movies each still photograph (each frame) is flashed in
front of your eyes for 1/24th of a second. This is why famous French
film director Jean-Luc Godard remarked, "Film is truth 24 times per
second."

        Each frame on a strip of film has a rectangular shape that is
projected onto the screen with a certain proportion. The ratio between
the width and the height of the rectangle is called the **aspect ratio**.
Early films used an aspect ratio of 1.33:1, which meant that the frame
was 1/3rd wider than it was high. With an aspect ratio of 1.33, if the
height is 3 feet, then the width is 4 feet; and if the height is 6 feet, then
the width is 8 feet. This is about the same proportion as a TV screen,
which might be about 15 inches high and 20 inches wide. Therefore, if
you rent the video version of a movie that was made before about 1950,
the film's aspect ratio will fit just fine on your television set.

        Most films made since the 1950s, however, are much wider
than they are high. The standard, conventional aspect ratio of 1.33 was
established in the 1930s and is known as the Academy ratio. American

films today typically have a much wider aspect ratio of about 1.85:1, and foreign films about 1.66:1. But sometimes an even wider aspect ratio is used. Some European films use 1.75:1, some 1950s widescreen films and 70mm films use 2.2:1, while others use 2.4:1. One means of achieving a widescreen format is to mask the top and bottom of the frame either during production of the film or during projection in the theater. Modern movie theaters use 35 and 70mm projectors that are so expensive and complicated they require a licensed projectionist to use them. If you see a film in which a boom microphone or other production equipment is visible at the top of the screen, the projectionist has not properly framed the movie. Complain to the theater personnel to have it corrected.

Another method of producing widescreen films is to use an **anamorphic lens** that will squeeze the images horizontally when recording them and will unsqueeze them when the film is projected. If such a film is projected normally, the images will be very skinny. The anamorphic lens is commonly used today. In Imax theaters, 70mm film is used but it is presented horizontally rather than vertically, allowing for a larger frame size.

Today there is a major problem because so many films are watched in video format on TVs. Since most contemporary films are in widescreen, they don't fit on a TV screen without some adjustment. So, modern films must be altered to fit the proportions of the TV screen. One common solution to this problem is called **pan and scan**. Using this process, the sides of the film frame are eliminated, cut off, and only central images of the film are seen on your TV. This means you may not be seeing the entire film as it was intended. This is a big problem with good films, since the directors used the whole frame to create their art and the pan and scan technique will not allow you to see the entire frame. With lousy films, it doesn't matter—go right ahead and watch them on your TV!

But with high quality films we want to see the entire frame the way it was shot. Another solution is called **letterbox**. In this case, nearly the entire aspect ratio of the film is presented on the TV screen with strips at the top and the bottom of the screen blacked out. With letterbox you see nearly the entire imagery recorded by the filmmaker, so naturally this is preferred over pan and scan. However, the problem here is scale. An image that was intended to be very large (on a big screen) is now very small on your TV. For instance, when Grace Kelly bends down to kiss Jimmy Stewart in Alfred Hitchcock's *Rear Window* (1954), her face fills the screen. In a movie theater, the effect is drop-dead gorgeous. On a small TV, however, this is a ho-hum moment. It

Grace Kelly in *Rear Window*

is too small to be effective. Still, with well-made films, if you can't see them on a big screen, it is better to have letterbox than pan and scan.

Since films today are regularly transferred to video for TV viewing, movie cameras have markings on their viewfinders so the cinematographer can see what will be included in widescreen and what will appear on the squarer Academy ratio for TV broadcast. Hence, today filmmakers typically plan for both formats.

Modern filmstock also has sounds recorded on it. A magnetic or optical recording is made along the edge of the film, near the sprocket holes. The magnetic sound system is similar to a cassette tape in which a magnetic signal is encoded on the film and read by the projection equipment allowing the sound to be synchronized with the visual movements.

Optical sound tracks record patterns of light on the edge of the film that can be converted to sounds by an optical reader on the film projector. They work much the same as the scanners used in grocery stores. The sound recording takes up some space on the filmstock, so the visual image is made somewhat smaller.

The technology of recording sound directly on the film, instead of using another sound source such as live music or a phonograph, began in the late 1920s. As a general rule, films made after 1929 are talkies, with synchronized sound tracks, although sound was often incorporated into films before that date. The exquisite F. W. Murnau film of 1927, *Sunrise*, used some sounds. For example, you can hear whistles, car horns, and even people talking in the background.

The first successful use of voices that were synchronized to mouth movements came in 1927 in *The Jazz Singer*, featuring Al Jolson. Between songs, he said, "You ain't heard nothing yet," which was a wonderful and appropriate statement to begin the era of sound films. It certainly is true today, particularly in light of Dolby enhanced stereo surround sound and digital sound systems.

Some critics argue that the introduction of sound was bad for the movies because filmmakers no longer needed to use visual images to tell the story—they could instead rely on dialogue. These critics argue that visual beauty and artistry gave way to music and voices. In fact, they're right. The early talkies were not as fun to look at as silent films had been. One of the concerns was that in the early days of sound films the positioning of a large, immobile microphone limited the movements of actors because they needed to be near the microphone. Some films from the early 1930s contain scenes of people sitting at a table talking into a flowerpot strategically placed on the table between them!

In many respects, silent films are superior and you should explore them. You will need some patience because you're not used to the slow pace and visual story-telling. But stick with it and it will be rewarding and educational. Try *Sunrise*, *Nanook of the North*, *The Wind*, or some German expressionist films such as *The Golem, Metropolis*, *Nosferatu*, or *The Cabinet of Dr. Caligari*, or try some of the early comedies of Charlie Chaplin or Buster Keaton.

Another concern is foreign language films. Just as with the aspect ratio problem, again there are two solutions to this concern.

The Golem (1920) uses expressionist design

First, subtitles can be added to the bottom of the screen that translate the dialogue into another language. Of course, reading the subtitles takes time away from looking at the visual images. Also, the subtitles obscure some of the images, and vice versa, the images sometimes obscure the words. Yellow subtitles help. Another concern with subtitles is that often the translations are not exact, which can be a stumbling block if the film uses lots of puns, slang, words with cultural meanings, or poetic language. A good example of the latter is the ravishing *Cyrano de Bergerac* (1990) from France. Fortunately, the English subtitles are extremely well done and they mimic the poetic quality of the French dialogue.

The second solution for foreign language films is **dubbing**, in which the voices are replaced with substitute actors speaking another language. If you've heard this you realize how silly it is when the actors' words do not match the movements of their lips. Often the quality and tone of the voices doesn't match the personalities either, and in addition, dubbing does not give the intonations and other vocal expressions of the film's actors. Besides, it's fun to listen to other languages. Because of these considerations, it is best to avoid dubbed films. There is an exception: Woody Allen had some fun with dubbing in *What's Up Tiger Lily* (1966) in which he completely changed the plot of a Japanese film, turning it into a very silly comedy in English.

Today, filmstock is available that can record either in black and white or in color. Modern technology even allows old black and white films to be converted to color. There is a major argument over the colorization of old black and white films. In general, film experts agree that this is a bad idea. If the film is any good, the director of photography was aware that the film would be in black and white and used that fact to aid the artistry of the film. Therefore colorization changes the planned dynamics of: a) light and shadows; b) shading that gives the impression of depth (called **chiaroscuro** in painting, Italian for light-dark); and c) contrast, the stark differences in brightness and light and dark images. These are the elements that give a black and white film its wonderful, unique visual look. After watching good black and white films you will eventually come to prefer them to color films in most cases. For example, it is impossible to imagine the exquisite, impressionistic *Portrait of Jennie* (1949) in color.

Before color-sensitive film was available, color was sometimes created in older films by either dipping the filmstock into a dye or by hand painting the frames. Different sections of a film could be dyed different colors, for example, to denote different locales, moods, or parts of the narrative. Color sensitive film was developed in the 1930s

The impressionist look of *Portrait of Jennie*

and several different color techniques have been used over the years. The standardization of color films began in the 1950s and today it is rare to find black and white feature films being made, but a joy when it happens. Some examples are *Kafka* (1991), *Shadows and Fog* (1992), *Celebrity* (1998), and *Pi (1998)*.

The filmstock is wound onto a reel that is then loaded into a camera. The camera has different lenses that can produce various effects. One example is depth of field, which refers to how deep the focus is. Sometimes the filmmaker wants only a near object to be in focus and the background to be blurry. Switching the focus from one image to another during a shot is called **rack focusing**. This is one way the filmmaker can steer the audience's attention to certain images on the screen. When near and far objects are in focus at the same time it is called **deep focus**. This technique was pioneered by Orson Welles and his cinematographer Gregg Toland in the 1941 film *Citizen Kane*, often judged to be one of the best, if not the best American film

Orson Welles in his masterpiece *Citizen Kane*

ever made.

Finally, film artistry depends a great deal on lighting, and contemporary films also often depend on special effects, both of which require equipment. Creative use of lighting, as in film noir for example, can add gloriously to a film's panache. Sometimes special effects can be controlled in the camera, but more often they are done after filming. One exception is the oft-used **process shot** in which, for example, the actors perform in front of a screen that has action or a background projected onto it. This is the technique that was used to show Indiana Jones running from a rolling boulder and is often used to show a landscape or background.

A good deal of equipment is necessary in filmmaking, but the next step is the art and craft of using the equipment to good ends.

The Production

Even small films today are group projects. A major feature film requires the efforts of hundreds, sometimes thousands of people. In this way, film is unlike other art forms, which are manageable by one or a small number of people. The cinema is a collaborative effort, the result of many voices and talents.

Production begins with a person known as the **producer** whose team is responsible for all of the fundamental and preliminary organizing. This includes raising money to back the film, hiring staff, arranging for location shooting, and so on. A **production manager** is responsible for running the daily operations and handling business concerns. The producer must hire a **screenwriter** to prepare a detailed script of dialogue and action. Naturally, coordination among many people is the rule.

During the filming process, the most important person is the **director**, who must take charge of the production and visualize and guide the shooting of scenes. The term "director," of course, comes from the theater. In some ways film directors are similar to drama directors in that they give directions to the actors. However, in the cinema the director has other important duties, such as organizing all of the visual components of the film. For example, the director works closely with the **cinematographer**, also known as the **director of photography** or **D. P.** The D. P. designs the shots and is responsible for setting up the lighting and the camera positions, movements, and compositions. The D. P. usually operates a camera and directs other camera operators. A fascinating documentary in which cinematographers talk about their work is *Visions of Light* (1992).

The director has assistants (**A. D.** s) to do most of the leg work and handle communications so that the director can concentrate on the major tasks of planning, setting up, and filming each shot. Some directors like to look through the camera; they care about the framing, lighting, and so on, while others focus more on the actors and the sets. Alfred Hitchcock is an interesting example because he rarely looked through the camera, though he cared a great deal about the mise-en-scene. Before shooting he meticulously prepared a **storyboard** (cartoon-like panels) that showed precisely what each shot should look like. The D. P. could then precisely make the shots according to the storyboarding.

After the shooting is complete, a good deal of work is still required. In the editing room, the shots must be joined together in a particular sequence and with exacting precision. This is the job of the film's **editor**, typically working in cooperation with the director. The sound tracks are then added to get a finished product known as an **answer print** or **composite print**. Then **distribution prints** are made and sent out to theaters.

The Structure of Film: The Shot

Just as a book is made up of sentences, a film is made up of shots. A **shot** begins when the camera is turned on and ends when the camera is turned off. Therefore, a shot is an uninterrupted, unbroken stream of images imprinted on a piece of film.

Just like a sentence, a shot can be of any length. It can be short or long or anywhere in between. Because of the nature of the filmstock and projectors, shots are made up of frames, therefore a shot must be at least one frame (1/24th of a second) long, but it could last as long as the reel of film in the camera will last. In fact, Alfred Hitchcock intended to make *Rope* (1948) a one shot film (like a book made of only one sentence) by obscuring the camera lens while he changed reels, so the film would seem like one continuous shot.

Time Code (2000) achieves this by using a digital video camera, in fact, four cameras that record real time (the screen is divided into four quadrants each showing part of the story). There are no cuts. In cases like this, reel time = real time! Obviously, in the vast majority of films, the story time is considerably longer than the running time. But, sometimes it's shorter. In *Night on Earth* (1992), about 35 minutes of events are shown in 125 minutes. *Stranger Than Paradise* (1984) is another interesting example. It consists entirely of a series of master shots with no montage, no cuts, at all.

Of course, most films use thousands of shots. The shower scene in Hitchcock's *Psycho* (1960) is only 45 seconds long, but contains 78 shots. A movie is comprised of shots, one after another.

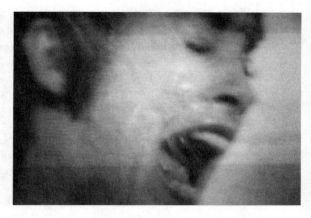

One frame from the shower montage in *Psycho*

Therefore, the shot is the fundamental unit of a film.

Film director Paul Schrader said, "You can think up a shot in five seconds—five minutes to explain it—three hours to execute it." In other words, each shot requires a good deal of time to be filmed. Suppose a filmmaker has a story or idea in mind for a film. How will this story or idea be conveyed to the viewers? Just as an author must think about the sentences that will convey the written story or idea, a filmmaker must think about the shots that will be used, their order of presentation, and the techniques by which they will be connected or run together.

The shot, then, is the basic unit of the film, and the filmmaker must design the shots, their order of succession, and the transitions from one shot to the next in order to convey the story or idea of the film. Here are the fundamental issues involved:

1. What is the subject to be filmed in the shot? That is, what should the camera be pointed at? This depends, naturally, on what we want to convey. Let's say our story or idea concerns a person walking down a street. We will point the camera at the person, and when we turn it on, the shot begins. When we turn the camera off, the shot is over.

2. How far away should the camera be from the subject? This is a question of **proxemics** or nearness. We can make an extreme close-up, a close-up, a medium close-up, a medium shot, a long shot, or an extra-long shot. Each kind of shot conveys a certain amount of information, and creates a certain feeling in the viewers. Which one is chosen depends on what meanings and how much detail the filmmaker wants to convey.

3. At what angle should the camera be relative to the subject? Of course, any angle can be used. We can put the camera directly above the subject (a **bird's-eye-view** or **overhead shot**), we can shoot the subject at eye level (straight on), we can put the camera near the ground and shoot up at the subject, a **low angle shot**, or we can put the camera on a crane higher than the subject and shoot down, a **high angle shot** (these terms are easily confused; it helps to imagine the camera being low or high when you hear low or high angle). Each of these angles creates a different feeling or mood in the viewers. For example, a high angle shot makes the subject look small and insignificant, as can often be seen in Hitchcock's *The Birds* (1976), while a low angle shot makes the subject seem large and foreboding, as is often used in horror and monster movies. We can also turn the camera cock-eyed so the subject will appear diagonally or obliquely in the frame, a so-called **Dutch angle shot**, which creates a dramatic, disoriented, or puzzled mood in the viewer.

4. Should the camera be moving or stationary? For a solemn, introspective effect, the camera can be placed on a tripod and not moved at all. Since the camera is not moving, the viewer is encouraged to scan the screen for information. A motionless camera forces more viewer involvement and is more commonly used in serious, philosophical, sad, or contemplative films. An alternative is to put the camera on a tripod or stationary support and swivel the camera. When swiveled right and left it is called **panning** (as in panorama), and when swiveled up and down it is called **tilting**. A pan or a tilt scans the scene (horizontally or vertically, respectively) for the viewers. Or, the camera can be put on a dolly that will follow a moving subject. This is called a **tracking shot**. The camera allows the viewers the perspective of following the movement of the subject. Or, a hand-held camera can be used that will give a slight jerky or flowing motion, giving the audience a feeling of realism, as in a documentary, cinema vérité, or a home-movie. A Steadicam can be used that allows the hand-held camera to move smoothly, without jerkiness. Each use of the camera creates a certain kind of shot that conveys to the audience certain ideas, feelings, or even unconscious assumptions about the image that they are seeing. Carl Dreyer's film *Gertrud* (1964) includes virtually no camera movement at all; it is very static and serious. Most viewers and critics are uncomfortable with that technique. One critic said that Dreyer's film was "A study of pianos and sofas."

In contrast, in Wim Wenders' glorious film *Wings of Desire* (1987), the camera moves about fluidly like an angel flying through the air—into windows, through doorways, above buildings, and so on. *The*

Cranes Are Flying (1957) is a beautiful Russian film that uses camera movement to create a feeling of dizziness and expressiveness that works very effectively. This film is also an excellent example of Dutch angle shots, which are used generously throughout the film. *The Last Laugh* (1924) by great German filmmaker F. W. Murnau was per-

The Cranes Are Flying is a beautiful example of camera artistry

haps the first film in which the camera was taken off its tripod and used as an artist would use a paintbrush. But, of course, such camera movement is sometimes not appropriate to the subject, meaning, or intention of the film, just as some paintings are well suited to fluid brushstrokes while others are not.

5. What else should be included in the frame with the subject and how should it be arranged? Should there be other people, objects, buildings, or movement? This is a problem of **composition** (the precise framing of the subject), and the choreographing of objects and actions within the shot, which is called **mise-en-scene**, a French term from the theater that means "arranging the setting." An empty frame can signal feelings of loneliness, separation, or alienation, while a lush scene conveys opposite feelings. The composition can be balanced or unbalanced, which also creates feelings and thoughts in the minds of the viewers.

6. How should the subject be lighted? The **key** light is the main light on the subject. Bright lights directly on the subject are known as **high key**, while subtle lighting is called **low key**. Other lights can come from the side, the top, or the back. Each type of lighting creates a certain effect. Film noir movies use light that comes from within the scene, such as a lamp (interior lighting), which creates deep shadows and areas of high contrast (dark and bright next to each other). Backlighting, as in *Eraserhead* (1977) for example, is often used to convey oddity, horror, or drama. Filters can be used on the camera to

enhance the effects, so for instance shadows can be created, rough edges can look smooth, and so on.

7. What should be in focus? The camera lens can focus on near objects while the distance is blurry (**shallow focus**), or the camera lens can bring both near and far subjects into focus at the same time (**deep focus**). Orson Welles' film *Citizen Kane* (1941) is famous for its use of deep focus. The camera lens also is capable of switching focus during the shot from one subject to another (**rack focus**) in order to shift the attention of the viewer.

8. What sounds should be included in the shot? Any sounds or music that come from within the shot—say the person walking down the street is whistling, or perhaps we can hear the person's footsteps—are called **diegetic**. Diegesis is a Greek term that means a "told story." In the case of film, the term refers to the world of events happening on the screen that are part of the plot and the action. But films nearly always use **nondiegetic** sounds, especially music. The sounds that are selected have a significant effect on the viewers—for example, certain kinds of music are commonly associated with mystery, suspense, romance, horror, and so on. One major problem is that nondiegetic sounds, particularly certain kinds of music, are overused in movies today and hence seem stereotypical, cynical, and manipulative, instead of being a genuine and integral part of the shot.

9. How long should the shot last? The meaning that is being conveyed will normally determine the length of the shot. Loneliness and alienation require longer shots, while frenetic action calls for a shorter shot. The shot may be part of a sequence of shots, known as **montage** (the French term for "assembly"), in which case the particular order of the shots is important and the length of the shot may be very short, only a fraction of a second. One form of animation uses stop motion, that is, a split-second shot is made, then objects are moved a small amount, then another shot is taken, then objects are moved, and so on repetitively. This is tedious work. The result is a series of split-second shots that are not perceived by the viewer as separate shots, but as a continuous motion. The animator can control precisely how many frames are filmed, knowing that 24 frames makes one second of film time.

Some theorists argue that the shot should last only long enough for the audience to get a glimpse of the subject then a new shot should appear, pulling the viewer along. This is common in modern films.

Others believe that a shot should last long enough for the viewer to contemplate everything in the frame, to think about the composition and the meanings, and to form some evaluative judgments and concepts about the plot. This idea forces the viewer to look at the frame, imagine, think, and soak in the imagery. Which technique is used depends on the intentions of the filmmaker and the decisions that are made should reflect the integrity of the art, not be manipulative or propagandistic.

   10. How should a shot merge with another shot? This is the problem of shot transition. At least seven transitions are possible:

Cut: In a straight cut, one shot ends and another begins immediately. This is the most common transition between shots. Viewers are so used to these abrupt changes that they do not feel any disorientation when one shot ends and another immediately begins. Normally cuts continue the ongoing scene or action in a timely manner, but sometimes the second shot jumps the action forward, that is, the second shot is considerably advanced in time from the first shot. Such **jump cuts** can be disorienting and therefore are more common in experimental or non-traditional works.

Match cut: Sometimes the action occurring at the end of one shot must match the action that begins the next shot. If the shot of a woman walking down the street ends with her going into a doorway, the next shot may show her coming into a room. The position  of the woman in the second shot should match her position at the end of the first shot. If a shot ends with her reaching down to pick up a coin, the next shot may show her hand on the coin. The shots match in action.
   Sometimes shots match not in action,  but in shapes on the screen (a geometric match) or in sounds, as in Hitchcock's *The 39 Steps* (1935) when one shot ends with a woman screaming and the next shot begins with the whistle of a train.
   Don't confuse a match cut with continuity problems. In *Vertigo* (1958) when Kim Novak is on the beach talking to Jimmy Stewart her scarf is in a different position from shot to shot. This is not a problem of match cutting, but a continuity flaw that film viewers have fun noticing. These flaws make it clear that shots are not normally taken in chronological order or immediately one after another.

Eyeline match: If a person walking down the street looks at a sign and then there is a cut to a shot of the sign, that shot should be made at the angle of the person's vision. If we cut to a **point-of-view** (POV) shot that shows what the person sees, an eyeline match shows the object at the angle of the subject's line of vision. If two people are shown talking to each other, the camera may be at each person's eye level to show us their point of view. Sometimes the shot shows the point of view of someone we don't see, such as a stalker, which is common in horror films.

Fade out, fade in: This transition has the first shot gradually disappear (fade out) while the second shot gradually appears (fade in). There is no overlap of the two shots. There can be any length of time of black screen (or any other color—one can fade to blue if desired) between the two shots, but it is most often minimal, not noticeable by the audience.

Dissolve: This is the same as fade out and fade in, except in this case the two shots overlap for at least some period of time, so that one shot dissolves into another. That is, there will be a moment of superimposition when both shots are on the screen at once, instead of a period of blackness.

Wipe: In this transition, a line or lines move across the screen pushing one shot off and pulling the next shot into view. The wipe can be vertical, horizontal, diagonal, or some geometric combination. This transition is rare in modern films, it was more commonly used in the past. The wipe is suggestive of experimentation, or a light-hearted, comedic, or playful approach.

Iris: Similar to a wipe, in this transition a circle or oval erases the screen then opens up to reveal another shot. The iris also can be used to call attention to details within a shot instead of cutting to a close-up shot. This is a rare tool in today's films but was used extensively in the past by directors such as D. W. Griffith. Therefore it can be used now as an **homage** (an honor or recognition) to older films or filmmakers.

Montage

Once the shots are recorded, the next step is to arrange the shots in an order that conveys the intentions of the filmmakers and allows the audience to perceive continuity of action and the meanings and emotions that are intended. The order of arrangement of shots is critical to this end. A crucial fact of film art is that a series of shots arranged in a particular way can convey more meaning than the mere sum of the shots. This is because the relationships between the shots also affect the viewer. The Russian film scholar Lev Kuleshov showed this effect dramatically in a series of experiments in the 1920s.

In one of these famous film experiments, viewers saw a shot of a man walking one way, then a woman walking the other direction, then the two of them meeting, then the man pointing off-screen, then a shot of the White House, and finally a shot of the couple walking up some stairs. Viewers interpreted these shots as one continuous storyline, although the shots were all taken at different times and in different locations and simply cut together in what Kuleshov called "**creative geography**." Because of the particular sequence of the shots, viewers mentally pieced together a logical connection between them and in their minds created the idea of a story.

Kuleshov's best-known experiment showed what is now called the **Kuleshov effect**, the power of one image to influence viewers' perceptions of another image. Audiences were shown a shot of an actor's face followed by first, a shot of a bowl of soup, then the face was followed by a corpse in a coffin, and finally the shot of the actor's face was followed by a shot of a child with a toy teddybear. Although the actor's face was the same in each case, viewers said the actor was expressing hunger, grief, or happiness depending on the juxtaposed shot. In other words, the actor's expressionless face was interpreted as showing an emotion relevant to the following shot.

This, of course, is a matter of perceptual and cognitive psychology. As Gestalt psychologists have shown, images that are near one another are perceived as belonging together. The important, astonishing fact is that an image can influence the viewer's interpretation and understanding of a subsequent or preceding image. This means that montage, the assembly of shots into a particular order, is just as important as the images in the shots.

In organizing the order of shots, filmmakers normally take shortcuts by using established, conventional rules for montage. For example:

(a) A scene normally begins with an **establishing shot** that shows the whole setting and the relationships between people and objects within the scene. Close-ups and other shots can follow and be intercut with the establishing shot. The overall shot is sometimes called a **master shot** or **sequence shot**. An interesting film experiment can be found in Jim Jarmusch's film *Stranger Than Paradise* (1984) because, as mentioned above, it uses only master shots throughout the film. There is no montage at all!

(b) The **shot-reverse shot** technique can be found over and over again in virtually every film. A shot shows us a person looking at something, then the next shot shows us what they are looking at. Alfred Hitchcock's films are good examples of the use of this technique. Also, conversations between people are good examples of both this and the first rule. A first shot shows us two people in a room. Then we see a close-up of one of them talking. Then there is a cut to the other person talking. Occasionally we see the master shot again to re-orient us to the action in the scene.

(c) Conversations between people make a good example of the technique known as the **180-degree rule**. This concept comes from the theater where the audience is always on one side of the actors and the action. In film, this rule keeps the camera on one side of the action so the viewers see the perspective only on one side of a 180-degree line. If two people are talking and the camera is cutting between shots of each of them, a camera over the left shoulder of one person is followed by a shot from over the right shoulder of the other person. In this way, the camera always stays on one side of the action, on one side of a 180-degree line.

———————————

So, to summarize, the shot is the integral, fundamental component or unit of a film. Each shot must be carefully planned and executed in order to artistically convey an idea, a meaning. Filmmakers must carefully arrange framing, composition, camera movements, focus, lighting, and other elements of the mise-en-scene for each shot, then must arrange the shots in a certain order, and plan what transitions to use from shot to shot. And too, filmmakers must consider how long each shot should last. Each decision has an influence on how the film will be perceived and on its ultimate meaning, the emotions and thoughts that the viewers experience.

The next chapter will discuss the meanings that derive from film and other arts.

Chapter Six

COGNITION & MEANING
The Illumination of Truth

"Art is the lie that tells the truth."
— *Pablo Picasso*

ilm can't exist without equipment and filmmakers, but film is equally dependent on the audience. As with all the arts, film exists in the minds of the perceivers. But perhaps more so than in any of the other arts, film is dependent on the acts of seeing, hearing, perceiving, and interpreting that are the products of particular functions of the human physiological perceptual system—eyes, ears, and brain. This is because the physics of film projection is not literally perceived by the viewer.

The Perception of Film

Because of the biology of the eye and the brain, a series of rapid photographs is perceived as a continuous, uninterrupted motion— a phenomenon called **persistence of vision**. You need an eye and a brain that work a certain way in order to perceive a film as a motion picture. Movie projectors are designed to flash still photographs (frames) on a screen at a fast enough rate that they will be perceived by the viewer as unbroken, continuous images that move. The movie projector periodically breaks the light pattern, causing the images to flicker on the screen—hence the common nickname for movies, "flicks."

The separate images, symbols, and bits of action that are projected onto a flat screen are interpreted and understood by the viewer as depicting objects, people, events, and even a story. The biological nature of our perceptual and cognitive systems enables us to perceive a movie—a series of rapidly projected still photos—as a coherent, integral whole. The eye and brain perceive something that is quite different than the physics of what is actually there. The brain perceives motion because of the temporal and spatial connections between the projected still pictures. This is why some people say that a movie is an illusion.

But this amazing fact is only the first wonder of the film medium. Equally fascinating is that the meanings (ideas and emotions) that are conveyed by the iconography (the visual images, their relationships and sequences) are created in the minds of the viewers. Of course, the meanings you get from a film are created in your brain. The meanings that are conveyed, the most important thing about a work of art, are non-existent without a viewer, and even more interestingly, are dependent upon the viewers' states of mind, memories, knowledge, experiences, and mental abilities. Naturally, a naïve child watching a film will not attain the same meanings as would a learned adult. This is a matter of what psychologists call **cognition** and only in recent years have film theorists moved markedly away from psychoanalytic theories (based on Freud's notions of the unconscious mind) and begun to embrace cognition as an important element in understanding how and why a film has meaning.

The Meaning of Art

Ultimately, when it comes right down to it, the most important thing about a film, or about any work of art—that is, the essence of a film—is its meaning, its overall, fundamental ability to touch us emotionally and intellectually, its ability to connect us with ideas, feelings, and insights, and to reveal truths about our lives and what it means to be human. A work of art, no matter what its materials, structure, or imagery, conveys meaning because of its connections to our world of ideas, emotions, attitudes, values, and experiences. In this way a work of art—no matter how well made—can be phony, shallow, inauthentic, manipulative, misleading, or downright dishonest. Or, on the other hand, a painting, a piece of music, a novel, or a film can touch us deeply and genuinely because it is honest and true to the human condition, beautiful, idealistic, and profound.

The meaning of a work of art is derived from cognitive processes in the mind of the viewer. An informed, knowledgeable, and thoughtful viewer has an advantage in understanding, evaluating, and profiting from art. Certainly **cognition** includes knowledge and ways of thinking, but it also includes and is influenced by desires, values, moods, recollections, attitudes, opinions, biases, and prejudices. You've likely noticed that sometimes other viewers laugh at different places in a film than you do, or that they sometimes reach very different conclusions and hold very different interpretations of a film's meanings than you do. In this sense, art is subjective. People differ in their interpretations of a work of art because they bring to it different backgrounds, knowledge, ways of reasoning, values, and other cognitions.

Although art is subjective, the artist must still strive to illuminate truths, sometimes universal truths or poetic truths, that go beyond a mere recitation of facts. It doesn't take a nonfiction film to convey truth. Many authors have made this point—that a work of fiction can often fill us with greater truths about the human condition than can nonfiction. A work of nonfiction that unflinchingly details one fact after another does not achieve the kind of truth we are seeking. Information and truth are not necessarily the same. The truths we seek go beyond detailed facts, they speak to our inner desires, values, commitments, sensibilities, and understandings of what it means to be human. In an interview in 1962, French director Alain Resnais said, "I find that as soon as we delve into the unconscious, an emotion may be born... I believe that, in life, we don't think chronologically, that our decisions never correspond to an ordered logic... I am interested in exploring that universe, from the point of view of truth, if not of morality."

With art, the quality of meaning, beauty, and sensitivity that is conveyed is the final, ultimate criterion of excellence. Of course, meaning is partially embodied in the quality of execution, and in the structure and the substance of the medium. However, a cinematic work can be executed flawlessly and still be a colossal failure—just as a book can be full of beautiful, flowing sentences, but still be dishonest, vulgar trash that does not express the poetic truths of life's mysteries and experiences. A film's images must be more than just well executed, more than merely accurate, realistic, or entertaining to the audience. The ultimate criteria of excellence, of value and worth, are the degree of honesty, sensitivity, ethics, and the depth of meaning that are expressed, inspired, and evoked by a work of art.

A good example is *The Seventh Seal* (1957) by Ingmar Bergman. This is not an expensively made film nor a film with high production values. Critics often complained about its cheap looking make-up and costumes, and the sluggishness and enigmatic quality of its story. However, this is a piece of art that can inspire us because it

A knight plays chess with Death
in *The Seventh Seal*

deals with honest issues of depth and wonder; issues relating to the meaning of life and universal questions about our place in this world, our hopes and fears, the nature of our relationships, and the ways that we treat each other. The images, the characters, and the allusions of the film rise above a pedestrian level for any viewer willing to look deeper than the surface content. In its metaphors, allegories, and suggestions one can find many nuggets of vibrant ideas and engaging emotions. In its ultimate meaning, it is a rousing success.

When a work of art is successful it is able to convey to its audience a meaning that is intellectually and emotionally honest, genuine, and true in spirit, a meaning that has depth, substance, and moral values that reaches our innermost hearts and minds in a way that is sensitive, moral and beautiful. For instance, a colleague of mine observed about Martin Scorsese's *Raging Bull* (1980), "People think it's about boxing. But it's not. It's about the experience of becoming a human being." Sometimes a work of art can touch us with its deeper truths, and in those moments it is a successful and valuable work.

Poetic Truth

Film, just as poetry, or any other form of artistic expression, can often be most profound, most truthful, when it deals imaginatively and provocatively (takes poetic license) with real people and factual subjects. Sometimes the best poetry and art treat the realities of life in a new way—with sensitivity, stylization, and a slightly off-center or disarming perspective that reveals something previously unnoticed, or inspires its audience to discover deeper, more lucid and genuine truths—poetic truths—about ourselves and our world. The recent film *After Life* (1999) by Japanese director Hirokazu Kore-eda aims at such heights. The film draws the viewer into a contemplation of life's defining moments by imagining dead people recalling their own past moments of poetic truth while a guide shows them filmed re-creations of their memories. In its best moments, this film aspires to the kinds of truths we seek from art.

A filmmaker whose films have often achieved a profound vision and a high quality of artistic excellence is German director Werner Herzog. During an interview with movie critic Roger Ebert at the Walker Art Center in Minneapolis in 1999, Herzog introduced what he called the Minnesota manifesto. He said he was throwing down the gauntlet to challenge films to be more honest, to aim for higher truths beyond simple realism, to aim for poetic truths.

The crux of his thesis is that TV and many films simply portray an empty, meaningless reality, what he calls "the truth of accountants." One fact after another (often violence, aggression, and other dispiriting images) is moronically paraded in front on us—meaningless bits of data disconnected from analysis or the substance of our emotions, our values, our minds, and our lives.

Herzog wrote, "There are deeper strata of truth in cinema, and there is such a thing as poetic, ecstatic truth. It is mysterious and elusive, and can be reached only through fabrication and imagination and stylization. Fact creates norms, and truth illumination."

In this vein, Herzog's body of work represents an artistic attempt at using the visual image, narrative, allegory, and stylized documentaries as tools in the search for "ecstatic truths." He views his oeuvre as one huge film rather than completely separate works, and it is easy to agree that all his films seem to chase the same awareness of life's mysteries.

Herzog's early films *Even Dwarfs Started Small* (1970) and *The Mystery of Kaspar Hauser* (1974) (which has the bitter German title, *Every Man for Himself and God Against All*) are good examples of his existential themes, and might well remind one of the

The search for ecstatic truth in
The Mystery of Kaspar Hauser

literature of Jean-Paul Sartre, Albert Camus, or Franz Kafka.

In *Even Dwarfs Started Small*, a group of prisoners has

escaped from their institution and are vandalizing the grounds in a progressively more and more absurd, chaotic, and uncontrolled manner. All the people in the film are inexplicably *dwarfs*—a fact that heightens the sense of incomprehension and bewilderment. The film somehow achieves a mystical, ecstatic truth that one could not imagine being attained by a film that presents a normal narrative. Herzog wryly observed that an understandable response to the film would be to wish that one had never been born! Of course, what he was referring to is the film's ability to capture and express the most outlandish, irrational, and absurd characteristics of human beings.

Federico Fellini's *La Strada* (1954) is another good example of a film that catches one off guard—one in which the ideas and emotions sink in long after viewing. Similar to Herzog's films, it attains a seemingly impenetrable truth in an almost fortuitous manner.

La Strada is ostensibly the story of a man who mistreats a woman. A viewer may easily become bored with its tedious details and meandering nothingness. But the pay-off is a big one for those who endure. At the end of the film and for some time later the film's meanings hit the viewer like a blast of emotion—stark and subtle poetic truths about the human condition. Similar to many of Ingmar Bergman's films, for example the intense study of a girl's mental illness in *Through a Glass Darkly* (1961), or the profoundly moving and mysterious *The Silence* (1963), or the emotionally dense and heavy *Cries and Whispers* (1992), the details of *La Strada*'s images and its narrative are transcended by the deeper meanings and allusions that endure long after one has forgotten the essential storyline.

Friendship is the theme in *Red*

Late Polish director Krzysztof Kieslowski is another filmmaker who aimed for poetic truths. His films, for example *Red* (1994), often play with the ideas of fate, circumstance, and coincidence. Are these fundamental truths or are they manipulative ploys meant only to amuse? With Kieslowski's films, a viewer is more likely to conclude the former, since the films present a subtle and sincere attempt at illumination rather than exploitation. This is the key factor in any art—its ability to touch us in ways that are genuine and true to the human experience, to illuminate fundamental truths, principles of aesthetics, or demonstrations of moral and ethical ideals.

Film scholar Jonas Mekas must have had this in mind when he wrote, "There is an area in the human mind (or heart) which can be reached only through cinema, through that cinema which is always awake, always changing. Only such cinema can reveal, describe, make us conscious, hint at what we really are or what we aren't, or sing the true and changing beauty of the world around us."

The Axe

Art conveys meaning through representation. When we look at a painting by Picasso or Van Gogh, of course we see lines, shapes, and colors. But beyond that, these elemental characteristics of a painting come together through their coherence, their relations, and their connections to form a perceptual whole, a unified perception. From the dots, lines, shapes, and colors, we perceive a face, a tree, a vase of flowers... or a purely abstract image. In any case, a painting, or any other work of art, has the power to transcend its own physical characteristics because the perception that is created has a context; it connects to our world of experiences, ideas, aesthetic concepts, our aesthetic ideals, or feelings. Therefore art can connote, it can elicit meaning.

Art can convey and inspire ideas and emotions that may or may not resonate with our experience, our knowledge, our sensibilities, our intellectual and emotional bases. It is possible at times that a work of art, through its integrity and its ability to connect with us in honest expression and inspiration, can open up a new world of ideas and insights. For example, a work of music is, of course, made up of notes and chords and rhythms. These elemental pieces come together in our minds to form melodies that can be interpreted and perceived by the human mind in ways that are so cohesive and structured and connected to our lives and experiences that they create in us a sense of mystery, adventure, calm, excitement, or trepidation—or they can inspire endless new ideas. Music when done right can move us, can inspire, and can evoke ideas and emotions.

Any work or art, including a film, because of the connotations and perceptions that it evokes can create transcendent meanings that go beyond the physical elements of the medium. Luis Buñuel wrote, "I strive for a cinema that will give me an integral vision of reality; it will increase my knowledge of things and beings, and will open to me the marvelous world of the unknown, which I can neither read about in the daily press nor find in the street." A high quality work of art has the ability to transcend its own raw materials, its own images, its own representations. It can connect with our world of ideas, meanings, emotions, and experiences. More so, a good work of art can open up new worlds—it can be Kafka's "axe for the frozen sea inside of us."

What counts about a work of art is its ability to inspire within us more honest, insightful, moral, and illuminating truths, to awaken in us truths that transcend the commonplace, that nudge our dormant emotions, thoughts, and dreams. Films and art that really matter are those that exhibit a humane and sincere sensibility, in fact, dare to be brutally honest and ethical rather than pandering to the basest of emotions as do such movies as *Pulp Fiction* (1994). The quality and importance of a work of art is ultimately determined by the degree to which its meaning is genuine, universal, ethical, unique, and insightful—and this also means true to the highest values, aesthetics and moral concerns.

Fortunately, some filmmakers are beginning to see the light. For example, David Lynch, whose previous work, though interesting and well-crafted, sometimes pandered to violence, misogyny, and crudity, has realized a more sensitive and poetic aesthetic in his recent film, *The Straight Story* (1999).

Does a film open up a new world of ideas for the viewer? Is a film ecologically coherent, does it hold together as an honest statement about the human condition? Do a film's aesthetic principles, its execution, images, stylization, and values represent something true, deep, beautiful, and idealistic, or are they false, manipulative, clichéd, and shallow? This is the ultimate appraisal of art. A work of art that is inauthentic, stereotypical, vulgar, crass, or exploitative, or one that promotes, exploits, or glorifies the wrong values, ideologies, or behaviors, no matter how well made, is a resounding failure.

Many, perhaps most, artists attempt to reach an honest, transcendent truth in their work, but, as Herzog noted, it is an elusive goal. Actor Anthony Quinn remarked, "The artist must be free. He can't be tied by rules. He leads. He leads the way up the mountain. He strives to reach the top. But others hold him back."

But it isn't so much that other people hold back an artist—although that is invariably true—the larger issue is the mysterious and evanescent quality of poetic truths. It is a difficult task to touch an audience genuinely, deeply, and uniquely. Only a few filmmakers have been able to achieve such artistry.

The essence of any art is its ability to convey a true, honest, moral, and profound look at our world and at ourselves. Unfortunately much art today is either exploitative, pandering, or simply aims to confirm the already held opinions and worldviews of its audience. If a movie critic dislikes a film, those who liked the film feel attacked, because it feels like an attack on their values and attitudes.

Audiences have come to expect movies to be exaggerated, caricature-like confirmations of their beliefs, biases, and world conceptions. This often means violence, revenge, and crass human motivations. If a work of art challenges or offers a new view of life, it is held suspect or outright rejected by today's audiences. But art has an obligation to challenge and to explore. Art must make us see anew, again and again. Art must show us the beautiful, the possible, the moral, and the idealistic.

Each art form has its raw materials, its medium, processes, and modes of production and creation, but ultimately all art should be judged by its symbolic, emotional, moral, and intellectual power to express and to communicate poetic and ecstatic truths and by its ability to represent aesthetic ideals such as beauty and art for art's sake, without exploiting violence, manipulating thoughts and emotions, or glamorizing immoral behavior.

Art must soar to the ideal, the honest, the thoughtful, and the poetic. This is the test of film.

PART THREE

Appraising

Film

as

Art

"Art is not a handicraft, it is the transmission of feeling the artist has experienced."
— *Leo Tolstoy*

*T*his final part deals with the ultimately important issue of how we can judge or evaluate film as an art form. Is film an art, and if so, is it good or bad art, a success or a failure? Should we view the cinema as a singular art medium—similar to painting, sculpture, drama, and poetry—or is film best viewed as simply another component of pop culture entertainment, similar to television or comic books? Is film art or mass entertainment?

These final chapters will give reasons to think of film as rightfully an art form, and also arguments against that notion. The first chapter of this final section, "Is Film an Art Form?" outlines the fundamental concept of what we mean by art and asks the reader to contemplate whether film fits into that scheme. Just what is art and does film fit the conventional criteria of art?

Chapter Eight, "Modern Art Movements," follows with a discussion of some of the most important and influential art movements of the twentieth century under the umbrellas of Modernism and Post-Modernism, and attempts to find a place for film within that context. Various art movements are discussed such as Surrealism, Cubism, and Expressionism, and a number of films are respectively considered as representative of various art movements, particularly within the Modern and Post-Modern concepts.

The final two chapters present the two opposing arguments, for and against film as an art form. Chapter Nine, "The Art That Isn't," takes the view that film has failed as an art form and is currently, like TV or cartoons or video games, a mass market source of entertainment, thrills, and confirmations of people's attitudes and beliefs, and nothing more. It is argued that the bulk of cinema history has provided essentially soft, fuzzy entertainment that is often disturbingly out of touch with the truths of the human condition.

The counter argument, the pro side, is given in the book's concluding chapter, "Film as Art," in which it is argued that the cinema is an art form that has provided a long list of genuine and illuminating works. This final chapter provides a generous list of films and filmmakers that have perhaps lived up to the potential of film as a high quality art form, or at least have made a valiant attempt. The argument is presented that certain segments of filmdom have aspired to and have succeeded in achieving the highest aesthetic aims of the fine arts.

Chapter Seven

IS FILM AN ART FORM?
Defining the Arts

"It's clever, but is it Art?"
— *Rudyard Kipling*

"Art is the only thing that can go on mattering once it has stopped hurting."
— *Elizabeth Bowen*

*T*he study of film is relatively new. This is because the cinema is relatively new. Nearly all of film history occurred in the last one hundred years. In fact, famous German artist and avant-garde filmmaker Hans Richter declared that "Film is the art of the twentieth century." Well, we know he got the twentieth century part right, but is film an art?

For many years experts have debated what is and what is not art, what is good art and what is bad art, what is the purpose of art, and what is the importance of art for the individual and for society. As you might guess, the answers the experts have provided have been varied and inconclusive, and have included the perhaps sensible notion that the question may simply be a matter of semantics that doesn't matter much. Still, many people believe it is worthwhile, enlightening, and interesting to attempt to understand what distinctions exist between what we call art and what we do not, and why it might matter to make such distinctions. Of course, to a large extent these are subjective questions, dependent on the tastes and values of the viewers, but perhaps we can find consensus for a few objective generalities.

People care about these issues and they find that some awareness and knowledge comes from the process of pursuing the answers— nebulous and subjective as they may be. Contrary to many people's opinions, art is important. We don't hear that fact very much in our society. The arts are much more revered, praised, and supported in other cultures, such as in Western Europe. At best, artists, authors, and poets are ignored by U.S. society, and at worst they are disdained, criticized, and looked down upon by the majority. Arts education is not given priority in this country. This is not true everywhere in the world; for example, in Hungary, high school students spend four years studying film and other arts.

Art is important in many ways. Look around your world and you'll see oodles of examples—graphic design is everywhere, and video, film, music, dance, photography, theater, literature, sculpture, and architecture pervade our surroundings. The arts are important also for personal satisfaction, whether you are a performer or an audience member. Here's an amazing statistic: More people in the United States attend arts events than sports events! Can you believe it? With all the emphasis that the media puts on sports, it is surprising to discover that attendance is greater at concerts, films, plays, operas, and museums.

Art is an important, even necessary, ingredient of our world. It brings joy, pleasure, insights, and sensory stimulation. Beauty, ideas, design, expression, and communication are all important elements of life and only available through the arts. As Marcel Proust proclaimed, "Only through art can we get outside of ourselves and know another's view of the universe which is not the same as ours and see landscapes which would otherwise have remained unknown to us." Art is important.

But, exactly what do we mean by art? What is art and what does it include? Although there are no perfect answers, we can make some solid generalizations. In a broad sense, the arts include:

1. The Written Word: Literature and poetry are important art forms that have been with us for many years and that have the power to amuse, inform, inspire, and express ideas and values. Literature certainly is an important art not only for the expression of style and form (found in both poetry and prose) but also as the inspiration for the contemplation of new ideas.

2. The Visual Arts: We normally think of painting when we think of art, but the visual arts also include drawing, photography, sculpture, and architecture. In today's world this also means graphic arts and multi-media computer designs. The visual arts are a wide-ranging and powerful means of expression and communication. There are certain crafts that may also be included within the visual arts, such as various pieces of ceramics, glass, wood, or other media that go beyond a functional purpose and express ideas and design concepts.

3. Performance Arts: The performance arts include dance, drama, and music. Theater is one of the oldest art forms and still thrives today in certain cities of the world. Music is as popular as ever. Opera is a dominant art form in many places in the world, although its audience is disappointingly small in the U.S. Performance is an integral means of expression and communication. However, not all kinds of performances are considered art, or at least not "fine art." For example, stand-up comedians refer to "their art" or to themselves as "artists." To most of us this is a tremendous stretch. Why? What qualities must something have to be called art?

Art is human expression, communication, and creativity at a high level not only of execution, but also of conception, intention, emotion, or sensibility. We do not call something art if its purpose is strictly utilitarian, entertainment, amusement, or necessity. Sorry, The Three Stooges are not artists. Of course, such judgments are subjective and arguable. However, an object or performance that exists solely for entertainment, practical, or mundane reasons is generally not called art. If it is, then we may conclude that it is bad art, poorly thought out, shallow, bland, insincere, unimportant, or inconsequential.

A cartoon, for example, is typically not deemed art because its style of execution and intention are purely for base amusement. However, some political cartoons and social commentary comics may lean over into the arts because of their high quality or innovative graphic design, their ability to provoke thought, or because of the importance of their place in the world of ideas and communication. There is no strict boundary between what is art and what is not. However, although the line is blurry, it is easy to find agreement in the vast majority of cases.

The cinema is a medium that combines many of the arts— drama, literature, sometimes poetry, photography, music, and so on. Therefore film certainly has the potential to be art when used properly. Film has some similarities with, and some differences from, the other arts.

Like literature and the performing arts, film presents a sequence, it controls time and space, and it is bisensory, involving both seeing and hearing. Like painting, photography, and drawing, film is a visual art that represents the world in two dimensions. Unlike drama, film cannot be live, it is recorded. There are many ways in which film shares properties with the other art forms. In fact, some film scholars have argued that film can in some ways subsume or include all the other arts. But to this day a satisfactory combining of all the arts has not been achieved. In this regard, we must reach the same conclusion today that

Sergei Eisenstein reached in 1946: "The problem of a synthesis of arts, a synthesis realizable in the cinema, has not yet found its full solution."

But cinema is more than a simple combination of other art forms; it has its own unique qualities. Film can be used to present images and ideas in ways that no other art can. Film has certain properties that allow a filmmaker to create what cannot be created in any other way, through any other medium. Here are some of the qualities of the cinema that make it a unique art form and differentiate it from other arts:

1. Unlike painting or photography, the cinema shows moving images. Eminent experimental filmmaker Stanley Brakhage even argues that film and photography are diametrically opposed arts. The photograph is static, designed, unmoving, and captured, while the cinema is dynamic, changing, on the edge, and meant to keep the viewer suspended and pushed forward, rather than stuck in time.

2. Unlike the theater or performance arts, cinema is a two-dimensional art that can be shown over and over again exactly the same. A play or a dance performance is unique at each showing, a film is not. A play can be presented in a number of different formats, for example the *thrust*, in which the stage projects out into the audience, or *theater in the round* with the audience encircling the action. A film always uses the common **proscenium** format—a flat screen with everyone facing the big white rectangle (except Omnimax!). Another difference is that a performance can't stop and try the scene again (though, that might be a fun experiment!), but film scenes are often shot many times before they are included in the final product.

3. Unlike literature, a film sets the pace, rather than the viewer. When reading a book or a poem, the reader can adjust the pacing. You can read slow or fast or stop and think. But a film requires ongoing concentration at a certain pace. Also, literature requires the reader to fill in all or most of the visual and aural qualities, while a film provides the sights and sounds. This is a major limitation of films, because they leave very scant room for viewer participation, other than being engaged in the plot. The visual images, the sounds, the music are all provided to the viewer. Imagination is not required as much in the cinema as in some other arts.

These are some of the ways in which film is a unique art form. But is it an art form of the highest integrity and quality? What is its place in the world of art?

A colleague of mine said, "If Shakespeare were alive today, he'd be writing for the movies." I thought: William Shakespeare a Hollywood screenwriter? Shakespeare working on *Lethal Weapon 8, Dumb & Dumbest, Hong Kong Chop*, or *Gulp Friction*? I find that very hard to believe—in fact, I don't want to believe it. I would like to think that a higher quality of artistic merit is possible from the movies than what we are now getting. It seems that movies give us only one possible artistic approach and style. All movies seem the same.

In a sense, today we get only one level of quality and phenomenal experience from the cinema. Yes, films vary in small ways from one another, but they seem much more banal and homogenous than the other art forms. Each movie seems essentially the same as the last—none of them exhibiting a very high quality of aesthetics. In music we have a wide range of styles (jazz, classical, country, polkas, rock, etc.) and varying qualities. The same could be said for the performance arts and the visual arts—but not for film. In film, it seems, there is only one approach—the commercial approach.

What if the other arts were like that? Can you imagine—what if all painters made only posters? Picasso paints the Spice Girls! What if musicians stopped playing classical music and jazz? What if they played only pop? What if dancers did no more ballet and presented only tap? What if sculptors made only Barbie dolls and figurines? There is a sense in which cinema has not lived up to its potential. There are very few films made today that exhibit the highest aspirations and executions of artistry.

Once there was a thing called an art film. But it seems to no longer exist, or at minimum it is very difficult to find. There was a time when artists used film as a medium of aesthetic expression, similar to literature. In fact, the same unfortunate thing is happening to literature today—there is entertainment (the vast majority) and there is literature (a rapidly shrinking art). Perhaps the same thing can be said of all the arts. Because of mass communication we have a world with less variety, a world more attuned to the marketplace and therefore to mediocre, mass-market opinions. It is progressively more and more difficult to find high quality art experiences, and virtually impossible to find avant-garde work in any medium.

Film's history does provide some examples of filmmakers who attempted (and sometimes succeeded) to make film an art. Most notable were Sergei Eisenstein, Ingmar Bergman, Jean Cocteau, Orson Welles, Fritz Lang, Federico Fellini, and several others. There was a time when one could go to a cinema theater and see the likes of *The*

Seventh Seal. Many filmmakers got their inspiration from such art films. But today it is increasingly difficult to find films that push the boundaries of artistry. Of course, there are exceptions. Werner Herzog of Germany continues to make excellent work, the Danish group known as Dogma 95 (including Lars von Trier and Thomas Vinterberg) has created some deserved excitement, Mike Leigh of England experiments with improvisational films about human struggles, modern Iranian filmmakers have updated the Neorealist style, and Peter Greenaway of England (a former artist) structures beautiful, esoteric films that involve abstract and complex subjects. But with these and a few other exceptions, movies today are a sad lot and it's difficult to conclude that they represent an art form of anything other than shallow, base, often objectionable diversion.

If film is an art, then why isn't it discussed in art books? If you pick up a book or magazine devoted to the arts you will not find any articles about movies. Considering the current state of affairs in the modern cinema, it is not surprising that films are excluded from art journals or art books. Instead, movies are written about in entertainment magazines, entertainment sections of newspapers, or in magazines devoted to entertainment or exclusively to film. Film has not entered the domain of the other arts in this regard.

When we think of the arts, we think of something beyond bland, uninspired entertainment. Has film lived up to its billing as the art of the twentieth century? Is film an art form? Does it represent the highest quality of art—has it lived up to its potential as an art medium?

The next few chapters will present the case for both sides of this issue, the pro and the con, film as a successful art form or film as a failed art. But first in chapter eight we will examine film in the context of the other arts, the Modernist movement of the twentieth century and its successor, Post-Modernism. Understanding the history of art and its various movements and their chronology will not only give us a more complete picture of the arts, but will help us contemplate and evaluate the proper place of the cinema within this scheme.

Then, the following chapter, "The Art That Isn't," will make the case that film has failed as an art, that the cinema is purely a commercial, mass-market enterprise similar to television, that it has neither allusions nor aspirations to fine art. Finally, we will conclude with an optimistic note: Chapter ten will provide an argument for the success of film as an art, including a lengthy list of films from throughout the history of cinema that can be viewed as high quality artistic works.

Chapter Eight

MODERN ART MOVEMENTS
Chaos & Cosmos in Search of Meaning

"I begin logically with chaos, that is most natural... The point as a primordial element is cosmic. Every seed is cosmic."
— *Paul Klee*

"The attitude that nature is chaotic and that the artist puts order into it is a very absurd point of view, I think. All that we can hope for is to put some order into ourselves. Insofar as we understand the universe—if it can be understood—our doings must have some desire for order in them; but from the point of view of the universe, they must be very grotesque."
— *Willem de Kooning*

"Art is about trying to make something out of the chaos of human existence."
— *Francis Bacon*

*M*odern art more than any preceding artistic style or aesthetic epitomizes the emergence of a cultural and social agenda, the revelation and celebration of meaning and statement—emotional, intellectual, and social—through expression and abstraction. Philosophical and psychological tenets undermine and pervade the artist's mind and brush. In the Modernist movement, scientific discoveries, psychoanalytic ideas, existential philosophy, photographic techniques, and other social and intellectual inventions exploded onto canvases, inspired dancing feet, and surfaced on film and page as artists attempted to capture meaning and order in a rapidly changing universe of seeming chaos.

Modern Art

The **Minimalists** believed that less is more, but eventually concluded that it is still not enough. The **Dadaists** exalted absurdity and incongruity, the art of non sequitur, in works that surprised, shocked, and steamed with anti-war and anti-society sentiments. The **Cubists** challenged the traditional notion that an object, a form, had only one true identity, one reality. Their works unveiled the multiple planes, angles, and geometric constructions that merge in the perception of an object. The **Surrealists**, reacting to Freudian psychology, approached meaning through expression of the unconscious mind and produced dreamy, fragmented, multi-media revelations of the hidden, the mysterious, the unknown, but perhaps knowable. Luis Buñuel and Salvador Dali said that in filming the seminal surrealist movie, *Un Chien Andalou [Andalusian Dog]* (1929), their technique was to shoot a scene until it made no sense! Out of nonsense arose a new, more potent, perhaps more meaningful sense.

Even the popular cinema has embraced the psychoanalytic/surrealist *modus operandi* in portraying the search for meaning from disorder. A classic example is Alfred Hitchcock's film, *Spellbound* (1945), in which a beautiful psychoanalyst (Ingrid Bergman) helps cure a handsome amnesiac (Gregory Peck) by interpreting his symbolic dream, the window to his unconscious. The much celebrated dream sequence was stunningly designed by Salvador Dali and vividly captures the quixotic bent of the surrealist mind.

The artist's ability to evoke meaning from image was also movingly demonstrated by early twentieth century German expressionist films such as *The Cabinet of Dr. Caligari, M,* and *Metropolis*. The style of an

A scene from the German expressionist film *Metropolis*

image became a means of affective and cognitive evocation disclosing an underlying meaning or order. In its many forms—paintings, film, prose, poetry, and performances—Modernism has emerged as an attempt to reflect, integrate, parody, and reveal a hidden order of self and world.

Primitive and prehistoric art adapted natural images, seeking truth through eternal, static, perceptively real, concrete forms, lines, patterns, and objects. Primitive and prehistoric art exposed the *retinal* truth. Art was adapted from nature, its images and its parade. The urgency was to find order in the chaos and cosmos of the practical, the natural, and to reproduce this order as it is perceptually organized. This philosophy was continued by representational and realist artists. But Modernist artists had other ideas.

Modernism yearned for cosmic truths beyond the retina; from within the psyche rather than the prairie, from the dreamscape rather than the landscape. When Hans Hoffman admonished Jackson Pollock to eschew subjective expression and stick to the natural world, Pollock succinctly, insightfully replied: "But I am nature." Ironically, it was Hoffman who later altered his approach and subsequently his work blossomed in intensity and meaning as it took on surreal tendencies.

Surrealists in all media provided a glimpse of cosmos from the seemingly murky confines of repressed, unconscious thoughts. When Marcel Duchamp's painted glass piece, titled *To be looked at (from the other side of the glass), with one eye, close to, for almost an hour*, was accidentally cracked, Duchamp insisted that the cracks were an integral part of his design and must be left in!

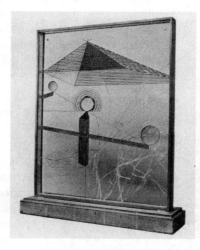

Painted and cracked glass piece by Duchamp

Both Surrealists and Dadaists used impossible, incongruent images to trigger truths and sentiments through metaphor, mistake, absurdity, spontaneity, and serendipity. At the other extreme, Andy Warhol and other Pop artists painted hyper-real images of soup cans and similarly mundane, ordinary objects, forcing the viewer to face head on the ultra-reality of common perception. The startling upshot of these two polar opposite approaches was that the Surrealist object was praised for it strangeness and the Pop Art object for its un-strangeness! Both lie on the continuum of chaos and cosmos, insidiously and seductively revealing aspects of humanistic, experiential meaning by lifting artist and audience to another plane of contemplation of self, cognitions, and the nature of objects and symbols in our physical and social world. Can a meaning-gestalt, an intellectual unifying concept, emerge from such paradoxically opposing views?

Sometimes words alone are not enough to express and reveal. Sometimes it is necessary to transcend language if we are to find meaning, to unveil order from chaos, and to dislodge and reveal gestalt from disorder. To explain art is not enough.

Modern artist Robert Rauschenberg expresses frustration, yet implies a contextual truth in writing, "I find it nearly impossible free ice to write about jeepaxle my work. The concept I planetarium struggle to deal with ketchup is opposed to the logical continuity lift tab inherent in language horses and communication. My fascination with images open 24 hours is based on the complex interlocking of disparate visual facts heated pool that have no respect for grammar."

The chaotic, tortured syntax of Rauschenberg's statement probably communicates his idea better than would a syntactically correct sentence and also reminds us that art is nearly always a non-literal mode yet still can impart deep meaning. From a chaotic sentence can emerge a cosmic (ordered) understanding and appreciation—a gestalt—which perhaps cannot be, or should not be, decoded linguistically. Similarly, meaning can be derived from non-verbal, non-representational art. Perhaps Picasso had this idea in mind when he said, "Everyone wants to understand art. Why not try to understand the song of a bird?"

Abstraction and Reality

An abstract painting by Kandinsky

The first totally abstract painting was created by Wassily Kandinsky in 1910. Art historians have reminded us what an incredible, courageous act of resolve and imagination this was. In his brief autobiography, *Reminiscences* (1913), Kandinsky mused, "In many things I must condemn myself, but I have always remained true to one thing—the inner voice, which set my goal in art and which I hope to follow to the last hour."

The audience, too, seeks beauty, understanding, emotion and integrity from the artistic performance or object. Both artist and audience seek the hidden, unspeakable truths from both chaos and cosmos in an inexorable dance of confounding attempts at synthesis, analysis, re-synthesis, and re-analysis. If words fail to provide the fullness of meaning, if words are not enough to express, explain, and reveal, then perhaps we should look to numbers!

In his book, *Concerning the Spiritual in Art* (1912), Kandinsky wrote, "The final abstract expression of every art is number." Number! The concepts and connotations of number, proportion, organization, geometry, and related mathematical concepts permeate the Modernist aesthetic. Paul Cézanne once suggested to a student that he look for geometric

Duchamp's cubist masterpiece *Nude Descending a Staircase* is both humorous and challenging

forms—circles, cones, cylinders, triangles—in the world around him.

The Cubists apparently took this notion seriously, and to its logical extreme. Marcel Duchamp's 1912 *Nude Descending a Staircase* stands as a seminal example of the Cubist deconstruction of object into geometric, mechanistic attributes. Yet it clearly retains an appealing and revealing gestalt! From the chaos of disparate parts, movements, symbols, shapes, planes, and fragments emerges a context for understanding, simplification, and order.

An example of a Cubist film would be Ingmar Bergman's *Persona* (1966), which presents varied perceptions of people, personalities, and reality. *Time Code* (2000) also attempts a Cubist view of narrative.

Relating and merging personalities in *Persona*

An abstract painting by Mondrian

Piet Mondrian's oeuvre represents the quintessential occupation with exploring the reality of order from the deconstruction of geometry, color, space, and time. Mondrian attempted to organize reality into the purest of patterns hoping to transcend the retinal world of sensation and discover a hidden world of intimate organization. Clarity and discipline were means to an end.

E. H. Gombrich in *The Story of Art* (1966) observed that in his pursuit of deconstructive truth, "Mondrian, like Kandinsky and Klee, was something of a mystic and wanted his art to reveal immutable realities behind the ever-changing forms of subjective appearance." Some films, such as the classsic Italian Neorealist and the contemporary Iranian attempts to capture the everyday struggles of daily life, represent a similar artistic intention. Their goal is to find and to express the fundamental and indivisilbe realities of life.

The Search for Truth

The search for immutable realities is one of the obsessions and defining qualities of Modernism. Those who have been lulled into accepting the common notion that "everything is relative" not only misunderstand the concept of relative (it may just as meaningfully be said that nothing is relative!), but also underappreciate the search for meaning in the roots, components, and insights that absolutes can provide in our mental reconstruction of the gestalt. In artistic expression and appreciation the absolutes are integral.

The point, the line, primary colors, right angles, proportion, form, shapes, perceptual principles such as interposition, linear perspective, figure-ground organization, reversal, and shape, size, and brightness constancies are absolutes that must be manipulated and re-manipulated in the search to reveal truths of both order and disorder.

In Mondrian's most influential essay, *Plastic Art and Pure Plastic Art*, his extremism and aesthetic purity were apparent: "One realizes more and more the relativity of everything, and therefore one tends to reject the idea of fixed laws, of a single truth. This is very understandable, but does not lead to profound vision. Art shows us that there are constant truths concerning forms. Every form, every line has its own expression. This objective expression can be modified by our subjective view but it is no less true for that. Round is always round and square is always square. Art makes us realize that there are fixed laws which govern and point to the use of the constructive elements, of the composition and of the inherent interrelationships between them. Art is the expression of true reality and true life, indefinable but realizable in plastics."

The Modernist approach can help identify the absolutes by challenging the conceptual mystique of ordinary objects. In *The Object Transformed* (1966), common objects are distorted and manipulated in unexpected, absurd ways. A cup is covered in fur; a book is inundated with pins, razors, knife and scissors; chairs are distorted, full of holes and wires; forks display tines bent in every direction; an umbrella is made of sponge; a burned mattress lies lonely on a barren floor. Similar challenges to the nature of objects are suggested by the exaggeratedly large, often soft sculptures of Claes Oldenberg—typewriter, french fries, electrical plug. The result is to throw the viewer into a state of philosophical questioning: What exactly is an object? What are its inherent and defining qualities? Where is the focus of order, of cosmos in this chaos?

Modernism is based on abstraction and expression. American poet Stanley Kunitz suggested that chaos could be conceptualized as the absence of time and space. The Modernist explores the chaotic world not through the concrete, but via abstraction. Spatial-temporal destruction has been celebrated and echoed throughout the twentieth century by authors, playwrights, painters, choreographers, musicians, poets, and designers. Well-known examples include Franz Kafka, Marcel Proust, James Joyce, e. e. cummings, William Burroughs, Merce Cunningham, Jean Genet, Georgia O'Keeffe, Italo Calvino, Mark Rothko, Jorge Luis Borges, Pablo Picasso, Gabriel Garcia Marquez, and John Cage.

Even punk rock music echoed the theme. The punks sought the essential and fundamental beat, tonality, and musical structure that epitomized rock music. Avant-garde historian Greil Marcus has chronicled this history in the marvelous book, *Lipstick Traces: The Secret History of the Twentieth Century* (1989). Marcus introduces readers to an underground of music, attitudes, style, and order (disorder?) that emerged from disparate forces within the Modernist context.

Similarly, Alex Cox's film, *Sid and Nancy* (1990) documented the rise and fall of the Sex Pistols' Sid Vicious, as well as the alienated, pathetic lives suffered by him and his counter-culture peers. Unfortunately, the film failed to even hint at the social and intellectual forces that contributed to the degenerate, languishing ethos portrayed. There may in fact have been more integrity in those broken, rebellious lives than in the social morass to which they were reacting. Art critic

Erich Neuman has pointedly noted that "In our age, as never before, truth implies the courage to face chaos."

The search to reveal absolutes is an attempt to deconstruct not meaning but an underlying reality, and then to reconstruct a gestalt pattern by manipulating the roots of reality into new realizations and patterns of emerging meaning. The process and the product stimulate cognition and meta-cognition of both world and self.

One of the most ambitious and deeply moving, even poetic, examples of the manipulation of numeric, geometric derivatives is the work of contemporary artist Jennifer Bartlett. Her work, *Rhapsody*, consisting of hundreds of squares of images, flows like music with a continuity and vitality that captures our imagination and turns our mind's eye toward the inherent power of lines, shapes, forms, and elements that when deconstructed create a non-linear emergence of gestalt meaning. The chaos of the moment, of the image, becomes the order of the mind, just as when blended tonal notes form a musical chord, or when unified images emerge from the independent, disparate elements of a mosaic. Unlike the Conceptual Minimalists, Bartlett's intention is to use the orderly structure—rules, mathematics, geometry, number— not as a means to an end, but merely as a means. Her work has its greatest impact not in revealing order in nature (or deconstructing reality), but in bringing order to the artist and to the audience.

The musical compositions of John Cage often share the same sensibility and directness. The symbolic, abstract rules and means of denotation can be expressive and emotive, touching viewers or listeners in mixtures of images, sounds, and meanings that create new awareness. The abstraction of order, of cosmos, extends our sense of time, space, movement, affect, idea, and imagination. Through compression comes extension. From derivative, the calculus emerges in abstract, non-linguistic symbolism.

Post-Modernism

Surrealism was a reaction to and affirmation of Freudian ideas—the uncovering of unconscious elements moving us closer to self-understanding. Dada initially developed as an anti-war attitude; artists were disgusted and chagrined by European society's inability to deal with contemporary problems. Structured society was viewed as meaningless and inconsequential. Absurd art was created to express a mocking disregard for rationality and the status quo. Dada subsequently subsumed a broad range of styles and media. Dadaists, Action painters, Abstract Expressionists, Pop artists, and New Wave filmmakers showed a passion for commenting on the underlying social fabric and the cynicism, ennui, stagnation, and disillusionment inherent in the struggle to relate to our selves and to our world-situation in a universe of unparalleled technological advance and information explosion juxtaposed against a social order still buried in barbarism and discord. Satire, parody, absurdity, stark reality, emotional catharsis, and abreaction became the working vocabulary in untangling social, moral, and spiritual truths. The Modern artist manipulated objects and concepts in abstract ways to produce cosmic or chaotic reorganizations of our philosophical constructs.

Flags by Jasper Johns

The evolution of the Modernist aesthetic reached a milestone with the work of painter Jasper Johns. Johns showed us the object as we had never seen it—the symbol as symbol. Flag, map, bullseye target, number. Eventually neither the object nor the representation of the object was enough, but the artist must next reveal the connecting tissue that seals the bargain between symbol and symbolized. A kind of meta-modernism. Perhaps this can be our signpost in denoting the beginning of a Post-Modernist expression.

Andy Warhol showed us the hyper-real, ordinary object (a soup can, a Brillo box) as art. To the pedestrian viewer Warhol's work

Andy Warhol's challenge to the definition and meaning of art

seemed like mockery, foolishness, and non-art, even anti-art. But to the thoughtful observer this work represented an awakening, a meta-morphosis, an important transition into a new realm of reasoning about the nature of art itself. Warhol's work required a new definition of art, a modified philosophy. The distinctions between object, sense, symbol, and meaning were being blurred and even doubted.

Some of Peter Greenaway's films, such as *The Pillow Book* (1997), also give the feeling of a new advance, a Post-Modernist world of art, expression, and communication. Perhaps the same aesthetic can be seen in the Dogma works, as well.

The oeuvres of Johns and Warhol evidenced a changing perspective, a new, slightly off-kilter glimpse at the world of chaos and cosmos. Abstract Expressionist painter Willem de Kooning echoed the dismay of many Modernists and Modern art connoisseurs when he said that Warhol was "A killer of art, a killer of beauty" (Danto, 1993).

The Modernist tack was fading and a new line of attack was evolving. In commenting on Warhol's *Brillo Box* painting, Columbia University Philosophy Professor Arthur C. Danto wrote, "It is the mark of Modernism in painting that painting critiqued itself. How is it possible for something to be a work of art when something else, which resembles it to whatever degree of exactitude, is merely a thing, or an artifact, but not an artwork? Warhol's object showed that the philosophy of art was going to have to be begun all over again, since the question Warhol raised had occurred to not a single philosopher in the canon of esthetics...it brought an end to a period in which art could be made in ignorance of its philosophical nature" (Danto, 1993).

We might well say that artistic works in the vein of Johns and Warhol heralded an era when the Modernist mode was giving way to a potent new Post-Modernist style, and with it, introducing an exciting new direction in philosophical perspective and interpretation.

Emerging Realities

From our cosmos we seek unity, order, sequence, relationships, connections. From ourselves we seek truth, beauty, peace, contentment, actualization. The Post-Modernist is thrust into a transition world where everything is challenged, doubted, even the symbol is nothing. Once symbols had meanings—pride, honor, love, obedience, duty. But advancing science, technology, philosophy, and social evolution have stripped the representation from the represented and denounced both! The medium isn't the message, there is no message! Does anything exist? Does life have meaning? Is everything futile? Perhaps in a future world there will be a new basis for hope and meaning, but for now the Post-Modernist cognoscenti find themselves afloat without bearings. Religion, myth, and all manner of truths have been questioned and found wanting. The Post-Modernist is naked, without the protective illusions of the pre-scientific world. Pre-Modernists might have warned us to clutch our illusions dearly, for they once meant our salvation. But it is our destiny now to realize that *dis-illusionment* is a necessary beginning for a new more honest, more genuine, more true emerging reality. As Erich Fromm warned: "Knowing begins with the shattering of illusions, with disillusionment."

Stripping the symbol from the object is an interlocking element in the still evolving and spreading disaffected, alienated, disillusioned state of Post-Modernist life. The cities, neighborhoods, and schools are rapidly becoming behavioral sinks, swimming in ennui and discontent, rudderless except for the constant allure of the dollar. But, there's no integrity in materialism. The individual, the thoughtful, introspective individual, is captured in a net of contradictory notions, fears, desires and values, without a floor, a focus, a solid footing. To fill the void, some people turn to the past and grasp at myths. Others embrace new age concepts or the promised hopes of ubiquitous new religions and quasi-political, spiritual, and philosophical organizations. But all are, for now, lost. The shift, the mutation from Modernism to Post-Modernism has begun.

While the Modernist challenged reality, the Post-Modernist challenges meta-reality. The Modernist's skepticism has become Post-Modern disillusionment. From banality to cynicism, apathy to violence, existentialism to deconstructionism, self-expression to selfish oppression, the evolution is apparent not only in art that shocks, ridicules, shames and insults, but resounds as well in the insidious interpersonal social world of individuals and institutions. A stunning example is Mike Leigh's film, *Naked* (1994), which successfully captures the decay, depravity, and violently pathetic manner in which the underclass Post-Modernist relates to self, ideas, social institutions, and other individuals. That such a movie has been written, filmed, and has touched such a large segment of thinking people is testament to a burgeoning aesthetic that desperately needs examining. Film Professor Amos Vogel has reminded us that, "...poetry and non-linear art are more suitable to the complex fluidities of the modern world view...Dissolution, fragmentation, simultaneity, decomposition—these are words in the service not of obfuscation but of clarification."

Other modern filmmakers have also echoed the theme of alienation, of chaos, of need for cosmos in a contemporary world in which myths are dissolving. The deepest and most metaphorical example is the trilogy by director Michelangelo Antonioni including *L'Avventura*, *LaNotte*, and the finale, *L'Eclisse* (*The Eclipse*) which is loaded with symbolism and concludes with a long series of empty, lonely cityscapes. Very, very moving. Wim Wenders' films *Wings of Desire* and the sequel *Faraway, So Close* also evoke the lonely, lost nature of modern life. When Cassiel (an angel) falls to earth (becomes human) he is faced with the universal conundrum of finding a way to be good, kind, happy, and productive in a disorienting, chaotic society. Wenders' **denouement** is presented as a combination of living life to the fullest (sensing, seeing, appreciating the ordinary) and finding hope in the knowledge that salvation may seem faraway, but is in fact so close.

Through a Glass Darkly

The films of Ingmar Bergman are also good examples of how style, context, and dialogue can portray the search for order in an empty, chaotic existence. In *Through a Glass Darkly* a family must deal with a young woman's schizophrenia. Her brother is dismayed by this confusing, torturous inner world of disorder. After witnessing a psychotic episode he emotionally relates his fears to his father: "Reality burst and I fell out. It's like in a dream, though real. Anything can happen—anything, Daddy!" This brief scene beautifully captures the lost, lonely consequence of floating disconnected in a world of chaos; the isolated, frightening awareness that "Anything can happen!" In Bergman's resolution the father assures his son that hope lies, "In the knowledge that love exists as something real in the world of men... Every sort of love... Longing and denial... disbelieving and being consoled... Suddenly the emptiness turns into wealth, and hopelessness into life."

No filmmaker has better explored the mysterious, ambiguous realm of memory than has French director Alain Resnais. In such films as the haunting, mesmerizing *Hiroshima, mon Amour* (1959) and the nebulous, oblique *Last Year at Marienbad* (1961), Resnais subverts time, awareness, sequence, and causality making obvious the seductive, elusive nature of memory. We discover that chaos pervades not only the outer, physical world but also our inner, mental life. The dreamy states of consciousness, the illusions of perception, and now the very essence of memory, our storehouse of facts and events, the nucleus of our identity, is subject to doubt.

The sardonic, care-less Post-Modernist attitude is more cleverly disguised by Hollywood producers who unapologetically dispense overwrought platitudes, simplistic violence, inhuman protagonists, and a paucity of ideas and values in vapid, innocuous commercial movies that more than live up to their moniker, but ultimately and profoundly burden us with an unending insult to our sensibilities. It is a troubling omen that the public is not more shocked and outraged by what passes as information and entertainment in the Post-Modern world of news, movies, TV, and the written word.

The Beyond

Modern art challenged our perceptions, our reality, and eventually our notion of art itself. It began with Impressionism, an artistic style that at the turn of the century was publicly scorned and judged as garish, homely, and unartistic. Ironically, among the general public today Impressionism is the most widely accepted style of art, judged the most beautiful, and adorns legions of living room walls!

The Impressionist artists were concerned with the relationship between light and object—an artistic form of quantum electrodynamics! This artistic philosophy reached its logical extreme with Pointillism, best exemplified and known by the work of Georges Seurat. Points of light and color, working in concert, blossomed perceptually into objects. Just as the musical notes of a literal concert merge into a symphony, Pointillism showed how a world of order could coalesce from the chaos of points. From dots emerge images.

From Impressionism sprouted limbs of progressively richer, deeper excursions into the meaning of light, form, movement, color, surface, and shape as myriad creative styles of expression erupted. Each style in its own idiosyncratic way projected the fate of chaos and cosmos—on canvas, in print, on stage, on film. It gradually became clear that the cornerstone, the glue that conjoined these disparate modalities, that bound and identified them, was the use and manipulation of abstraction as a means to insight and expression. Each medium and style explored this new territory in its own moment of truth.

The rich colors of the Fauves, the surprise, incongruity, and shock of the Dadaists, the illusion and deception of the Op and Kinetic Artists, the dreamy worlds of the Surrealists, the fragmented planes of the Cubists, the plastic search for absolute laws by the de Stijl artists, the mundane and ironic reality-mirrors of Pop Art, the loneliness and introspection of Minimalism, the subjective honesty of Abstract

Expressionism—each in its own manner contorted and extended not only the reality of objects but also the more tantalizing mental world of ideas and concepts in an abstraction of perception, thinking, and reality. Perhaps the inevitable result of this exploration was the emergence of an artistic philosophy ready to explore, challenge, and deconstruct even the essence, the ultimate meaning of abstraction itself.

The social, emotional, and cognitive shock waves of this adventure are now rippling and blending with the social and cognitive consequences of parallel scientific advances, in particular those disarming, unsettling, provocative ideas arising from contemporary biology, physics, and cosmology. The emerging Post-Modern zeitgeist, although disturbing in many respects, may prove to be the necessary path to a new enlightenment, to freedom from the constraints of the literal and subjectively perceived reality, and an entrance into a meta-conscious aesthetic.

The dissolution of myth, of perceptual reality, the decay of symbol, leaves the individual without substance, without security. Each artist, each filmmaker has attempted an answer. But none of the resolutions has established a resonance with the mood of our times. The Post-Modern ethos still languishes unattached, lonely, without anchor. What is the meaning of life? How should we live? Can art provide some meaning, some truth, some comfort? When object, image, perception, memory, and symbol have been doubted and dismantled, what immutable reality persists?

Chapter Nine

THE ART THAT ISN'T
The Severed Head of Cinema

"The movie represents commercialism that has gone so far into intensity for intensity's sake that it becomes a minority taste...it casts a slimy-naughty spell."
— movie critic Pauline Kael

No one takes film seriously. Perhaps that's just as well, since film is the only art medium that has no subdivision devoted to the expression of fine arts. Film is the only art form that is utterly devoid of art.

The film medium is devoted exclusively to mass culture entertainment. Its ultimate goal, naturally, is money—money at any and all costs. Pulitzer Prize-winning playwright Sam Shephard expressed his disdain for Hollywood stating, "They'd get a hockey player to direct a film if they'd think it would sell."

The Two Heads of Art

Other art forms—dance, music, painting, sculpture, photography, etc.—are dichotomous enterprises. On the one hand, each of these arts has a mass culture branch that churns out cheesy wildlife paintings, figurines, prints of flowers and landscapes you can pick up at K-Mart, top 40 music, State Fair trinkets, sci-fi novels, Leroy Nieman splotches of sports heroes, and so on.

But on the other hand, there are branches of painting, sculpture, music, dance, and all other arts—except film—in which practitioners and their audiences can struggle and experiment with the challenge of depicting, expressing, and communicating the highest and purest artistic explorations of form, content, style and creativity.

A refined and educated person, with some effort, can find honest, thoughtful, contemplative, reflective, and sometimes even progressive or experimental pieces of two- or three-dimensional art, literature, poetry, or performances in theater, dance, or music. Even in architecture we occasionally find a compelling or creative piece of work sprouting within our communities. Consider I. M. Pei's works in Paris, Hong Kong, and Washington, D.C., Frank Gehry's buildings in Minneapolis and Prague, the new Getty center in Los Angeles, the Guggenheim, and many more. Sculptures of fine art status are prolific in European cities such as Paris, Rome, and Berlin, and can even be found in some U.S. cities such as Chicago, Portland, Minneapolis, New York, Seattle, and San Francisco.

While the mass culture has MTV, action figures, popular music, romance novels, and the like, the fine arts fortunately are represented in some quarters and to some degree. The performance arts are not exactly thriving, but every major city offers venues for creative works in music, theater, dance, and sometimes performance art. Particularly interesting are the latest experimental works that use mixed media, such as theater with holovision, puppetry or video, and creations that merge dance, opera and music, such as the works of Philip Glass and Robert Wilson.

Of course, outlandish, tacky Broadway shows are readily available, but a motivated theatergoer can find more profound, visionary, and delicate performances offered periodically. Yes, we have pop and country music, but we also have classical, opera, jazz, and some experimental compositions. Certainly we are inundated with atrocious video and graphic arts, but we can also find more refined, transcendent works or edgy, experimental pieces of painting, photography, prints, and drawings.

Not so in film. Of all the fine arts, film has been left behind, dumped into the category with black velvet paintings, polkas, and video games, discarded to the heap of bland, puerile, and derivative mass culture pabulum that is spoon-fed to audiences unaware of its inauthenticity and its mind- and soul-numbing enervating qualities. What is astounding is that anyone goes to movies anymore. They certainly wouldn't if they took film seriously.

Film's Failure

The film medium is not taken seriously by filmmakers or by audiences. Perhaps there is no avant-garde in any art medium any longer. That is arguably because pop culture has homogenized us into nearly identical automatons. But the lack of experimentation and risk-taking in the cinema is frightening. Here is a medium that seems to have such great artistic potential—the expression of the moving image. One would think that film as a medium presents creative artists with a grand opportunity for something other than exploiting audiences, advertising products, and creating promotional tie-ins with fast-food chains in order to make an easy buck.

No one even talks much about films anymore. All that is ever said is whether one liked it or not, whether it was "good," and a description of the plot. About as far as anyone goes in analyzing a film is to talk about the errors of continuity they noticed and whether they felt the movie was realistic or entertaining. French director Jean-Luc Godard once said, "I'd like to stop the picture between reels so the audience could discuss the points made." But who does he think is in the audience, and what would they have to say? Perhaps if the points of the film were explained to them first, it would be a beginning. In fact, there isn't much to say about most movies because they are so superficial and vulgar. What if films lived up to their potential as art forms?

One would think that films could at minimum be windows on the state of our existence, or could provide some cogent insights into our social, political or aesthetic concerns. But instead movies give us a vacuous and myopic picture of the world. Portuguese filmmaker Manoel de Oliveira observed, "American films that glorify sex and violence are based on the ancient feeling of vengeance...At the end the victim is saved and the punishment falls on the persecutor and the viewers leave the cinema convinced there is justice in the world. It's a false construction to simulate justice in a world of injustices."

The cinema constantly infects its audiences with such trite and pernicious messages. But audiences don't seem to notice. No one complains! In the 1960s, the New York film group known as Cinema 16 had over nine thousand members. Today it would be difficult to find one hundred cinephiles who will take film seriously, who will discuss and evaluate its nuances, ideological messages, and structural form. What *could* films be?

What about creative self-expression, artistic vision, depiction of the human condition, and commentary on social, philosophical and aesthetic issues? What about art for the sake of communication, provoking thought, and revealing subtlety, mystery, and insight? What about art as explorer of the boundaries of form and style?

Spanish director Francisco Regueiro argued that "A film must be alive. When this happens, it smashes, devours, pulverizes any synopsis, plot, story. It speaks, talks, and explains itself. It constantly changes itself, its characters weave in and out of the screen. Their performance is different at each screening." Similarly, surrealist filmmaker Luis Buñuel suggested the potential of the medium: "In the hands of a free spirit, the cinema is a magnificent and dangerous weapon. It is the superlative medium though which to express the world of thought, feeling, and instinct."

But modern movies give us a never-ending parade of soft-core propaganda, selling the most sophomoric attitudes, beliefs, values, and stereotypes *ad nauseam*, without the slightest evidence of thoughtfulness, parody, or depth of analysis by either filmmaker or film viewer. It is not just products that are placed in the frames of the latest Hollywood spectacles, but also attitudes, values, ethics, and pop psychology permeate the screen. Along with your *Star Wars* action figures you also get lessons on war, justice, and gender roles.

German film director Wim Wenders observed, "I think entertainment films are the real political films these years. Because they are one big advertisement for the status quo. *Star Wars* is the most political film...I wouldn't say it's fascist, but you can see it as a tribute to Leni Riefenstahl. The ending is like a quotation from her *Triumph of the Will*, a film about the Nazis. You like to not admit it had a very dangerous aspect. That's what happens when you watch *Star Wars*. I had the same feeling of being overwhelmed and not wanting to admit there are implications I would call dangerous. To me, *Star Wars* makes a clear statement on American entertainment culture...It gives a highly ideological notion of the world, a totally artificial and false picture. It has nothing to do with how the world really is."

Unfortunately the mass media, including TV news programs and newspapers, jump on the bandwagon and daily list the gross monetary income of current films and give daily unpaid advertisements for such films as *Star Wars* and the multitude of toys, fast food, and other garbage that go with them.

On the Head of a Pin

Film critics don't take films any more seriously than anyone else. On the contrary, they symbiotically peddle the same pabulum—

like teenagers discussing the latest fashion trends. In fact, the latest trend is for local TV newscasters, particularly huckleberry sports announcers and Barbie weather dolls, to tell us which movies to see. I suppose that's only fair since Oprah Winfrey tells us which books to read.

Critics are not legitimate analysts of film, but are merely part of the entertainment package. The recent scene-by-scene re-make of *Psycho* (1998) should have been received by a critic's word-by-word copy of one of the original 1960 reviews, only in a different font. Who would notice? Film critics proffer their prosaic, stale, off the cuff opinions about plot, characters, and shallow celebrities without any hint of nuance, depth of analysis, or proper critique of what the commercial and cultural messages are in movies.

Movies both reflect and shape the mass, popular culture. They are insidious in their unyielding, pervasive propaganda. Their messages are powerful partly because they are so consistent from film to film. We learn how to talk, how to dress, how to love, when to fight, when and whom to kill, who our enemies are (Communists, Arabs, American Indians, etc.), and our class and gender stereotypes. Yet, you would never think any of this mattered by listening to a film reviewer. Critics talk about the movies the way one would talk about a Stephen King novel, a Madonna song, a new Chevrolet, a football game, or a hamburger.

But you might ask, don't the Academy Awards take film seriously? You've got to be kidding! The Oscars are nothing but shameless self-promotion in which the very perpetrators of movie trash award each other with statues and ridiculous, embarrassing accolades. The viewing public roots for their favorites apparently without a clue that the winners are not honored for excellence but for popularity within the industry. It's all part of the entertainment and advertising package. The Academy Awards are a clever marketing tool. Like the Spice Girls, it has nothing to do with art.

What about film studies? Yes, you can take courses on film history, analysis, and theory at universities. But even in that academic setting you are likely to find that your textbook has a picture of *Forrest Gump* (1997) on its cover and that you are writing a paper on *The Return of the Jedi* (1983). Would one expect similar circumstances in a college course on literature (study of romance novels), poetry (Rod McKuen), or music (Hootie and the Blowfish)? Film students should demand a refund of their tuition. Such film studies should not be portrayed as equivalent to the study of literature or art. These studies relegate film to the other forms of mass entertainment, such as television, and they are properly studied not as art forms but as influential and

informative components of a society. For example, we might rightfully ask: What effect does this pervasive assault have on us?

When history judges artistic excellence, certain names will not
be ignored. Mozart, Kandinsky, Chekhov, Rembrandt, Shakespeare,
Rodin, James Joyce, Frank Lloyd Wright, Michelangelo, Van Gogh, and
so many more—but, you get the idea. The arts are two headed. One
head looks to the masses, to base entertainment, to money. The other
head aims at higher pursuits, to aesthetics, to mystery, paradox, and
ambiguity, to depth of reason and emotion, to the human condition.
Where is film in this scheme? What filmmakers have given their best
to art? Perhaps Ingmar Bergman, Sergei Eisenstein, Jean-Luc Godard,
Federico Fellini, and the directors of Dogma 95 from Denmark, maybe
John Ford, Michelangelo Antonioni, Fritz Lang, Alain Resnais, Luis
Buñuel, Chris Marker, and Orson Welles—perhaps even Alfred
Hitchcock. But even these great masters can only marginally be called
the greatest of artists because most (if not all) of their works were produced primarily as entertainment for the masses, and rarely did they
push the limits of the artistic undertaking. To a large extent, while their
films surely stand far above the crowd, even these directors are pre-
dominantly mainstream in that their films followed traditional form and
narrative structure.

In film we rarely find exploration of the possible. Filmmakers
such as Maya Deren, Kenneth Anger, Michael Snow, Bruce Conner,
Stanley Brakhage, and Chantal Akerman have made some inroads into
the realm of the possible in celluloid, but obviously their works are not
well known and have not risen to the level of cultural consciousness as
is the case of artists such as those mentioned above. How would they?
Where would one go to see their work, read analyses of their ideas, or
discuss their impact? One can see paintings, hear concerts, attend theater, opera, and dance performances, but where does one enjoy and
learn from cinema art? Let's go see the Ron Rice flick at the mall's
Cineplex 36? The answer of course is nowhere. There is no art in film.

The movies with which we are stuck are not only lacking in the
aesthetics of fine art, but in addition, as if to rub salt in the wounds, they
insult, degrade and dehumanize us with their incessant and insidious
fluff, melodrama, violence, clichés and stereotypes. The illustrious
Orson Welles lamented, "You could write all the ideas of all the movies,
mine included, on the head of a pin. It's not a form in which ideas are
very fecund, you know."

In the influential book *From Caligari to Hitler* (1947) culture
critic Siegfried Kracauer argued that an examination of movies can tell
a great deal about the values of the society that produces and supports
them. Kracauer reasoned that an analysis of German expressionist films

of the 1920s and 1930s would provide helpful insights into the ethics and nature of the society that bred and nurtured Nazism. Well, what do today's Hollywood films say about us? Are we obsessed with unsophisticated, simple-minded, macho, vengeful, homophobic, and violent solutions to every problem? Are some people irredeemably bad? Do they need to be killed? Is nearly everyone in the mob or on the police force? Why is it funny when a person's head is blown off? Why does the image of a dog or a child invariably elicit heartfelt "ooohs" and "aaahs" from the audience? How is it that there is a genre known as "gangster" films? Are there gangster paintings, gangster operas, or gangster sculpture? Of course, rap music is the appropriate equivalent. This is where we're at in the world of film.

Pop Culture's Guillotine

The superficial and propagandistic content of the modern cinema would give concern to any thinking person—if such things were taken seriously. But art lovers should be even more discouraged by film form. Every modern movie appears to have been robotically stamped-out of some Hollywood machine, programmed according to some unrelenting, moronic formula in order that every movie will have precisely the same lame, tired format and look.

Sadly, even independent films today are indistinguishable from studio trash. How is it that audiences don't notice the silly contrivances, the artificial, irrelevant techniques, and the predictable form? How is it that they don't revolt? The helicopter shots, the mood music, the exploitation of every human emotion (particularly vengeance), the one-dimensional characters, the predictable plots and tidy resolutions, swirling cameras, clear, sweeping panoramas of glistening landscapes, sexy women, older men, car chases, exploding things, and juvenile dialogue. Oh, and guns. It wouldn't be a movie if there weren't a gun. Today, it's sad to say, one could watch a movie with eyes closed.

Isn't it sad how easily people are influenced—how easily young people have accepted the sales pitches, how they proudly show their allegiance to big business (to money) by wearing company logos on their clothes, how they spout the greedy, short-sighted attitudes they've absorbed from legions of hours in front of the twin screen gods, TV and movies? Like sponges without brains, the masses soak up the non-stop deluge of pedestrian prattle without the slightest critical ear or eye.

From classrooms to board rooms to voting booths (yes, a professional wrestler was elected Governor of Minnesota and other celebrities have regularly been elected by voters) to living rooms to relationships to families to our own inner psyches, we are engulfed by society's total surrender to the values and ideals of a celebrity-worshiping popular culture. Where can one escape the omnipresent saturation of TV sitcoms, pulp novels, talking heads, shopping malls, swimsuit editions, late night TV ala Letterman and Leno (who are nothing but shills for extreme right-wing propaganda, hucksters, and advertisers), entertainment news (*Network*, 1976, doesn't seem like a parody anymore), talk radio, sports-worship (I wanna be like Mike), video games, internet wastelands, vapid celebrities, more celebrities, advertisers (swoosh) and worst of all, Hollywood movies? Today one must listen very carefully to hear the sublime, plaintive note of artistry amidst the cacophony of modern movies. Some say that it can't be heard anymore.

The arts have always been a two-headed monster. We likely will always have a schism between mass culture entertainment and serious, aesthetic exploration. In the cinema, some critics and scholars have taken to using the terms movie and film to distinguish between the two enterprises. A movie is made for entertainment (i. e., profit) only, while a film has purposes of artistry, communication, expression, and so on. In literature, the artistic component is still present, but it is rapidly fading, is on its last legs. Have you been to a bookstore lately? Will literature and poetry soon lose their fine art head and join film as one-dimensional arts—art forms lacking art?

In her 1996 essay "The Decay of Cinema," noted author Susan Sontag mused on the end of art in film. She wrote, "Films made purely for entertainment (that is, commercial) purposes, are astonishingly witless; the vast majority fail resoundingly to appeal to their cynically targeted audiences... The reduction of cinema to assaultive images, and the unprincipled manipulation of images (faster and faster cutting) to make them more attention-grabbing, has produced a disincarnated, lightweight cinema that doesn't demand anyone's full attention... Cinephilia has no role in the era of hyperindustrial films... If cinephilia is dead, then movies are dead too."

Who will write the eulogy for literature?

In *The Sane Society* (1955) psychologist and social philosopher Erich Fromm surveyed the state of United States society and concluded that it was insane. Forty some years later the patient is no better, and in fact now seems beyond the hope of therapy. Popular culture has ruined nearly everything, including the cinema. No one takes film seriously. Maybe that's just as well. But on the other hand, maybe it's time that someone did.

Chapter Ten

FILM AS ART
Excellence in Cinema

"Film is the art of the twentieth century."
— Hans Richter, 1971

"You can be grateful that my invention is not for sale, for it would undoubtedly ruin you."
— Auguste Lumière, 1895

"It isn't worth it."
— Thomas Edison's reply when asked if he wanted to copyright the Kinetoscope in England and France, 1891

*T*he sentiment of some early filmmakers that cinema had no future seems ironically humorous in light of today's international output of films and the industry's huge budgets and profits. But a critical look at how far we have come and what has been accomplished adds some spice to that sentiment, and perhaps a tinge of veracity. Still, there is a large body of work in film that can be said to represent the ideals and aesthetics of fine art, works that attain a singular, poetic meaning and inform us with their honesty, beauty, and integrity. Here is a generous look at some of cinema's best work.

Realism

Many of today's films are in tune with the artistic idea of Realism—show the world as it is—and many films have achieved greatness in this style. The concept is best exemplified by documentaries, particularly direct cinema or cinema vérité, in which the filmmaker tries to record events with as little interference as possible. Excellent modern examples include the films of Frederick Wiseman (consider *Titicut Follies*, 1967, a film that was banned because of its honest portrayal of the dehumanizing conditions inside a criminal mental institution); *Le Sang Des Bêtes* (1949), an unflinching, eye-opening look inside a slaughter house; *The Sorrow and The Pity* (1970), a moving portrait of anti-Semitism during the Nazi occupation of France; the definitive Holocaust film, *Shoah* (1985), over nine hours long, mostly interviews; *Hearts and Minds* (1974), perhaps the best film about Vietnam; *Far From Vietnam* (1967), an acclaimed critical melange from several French directors; *Hearts of Darkness* (1991), which chronicles the making of *Apocalypse Now* (1979), the most audacious film about Vietnam; *The Mystery of Picasso* (1956), an intimate look at the artist and the creative act; *The Atomic Café* (1982), a hilarious and harrowing collage of clips of government propaganda films about "the bomb"; *Koyaanisqatsi* (1983) with music by Philip Glass, a non-narrative topological light show; *Working Girls* (1987), Lizzie Borden's polemic on the politics of prostitution; *Brother's Keeper* (1992), the riveting, unbelievable tale of backwoods brothers accused of murder; *When Billy Broke His Head* (1995), the best film on activism and attitude among disabled people; and finally, the musical documentaries *Monterey Pop* (1968), the first big rock concert film; *Sweet Toronto* (1969) featuring a surprise visit by John Lennon and Yoko Ono; *Gimme Shelter* (1970), a look at the Rolling Stones; and *Don't Look Back* (1967), which documents Bob Dylan's tour of England.

Although not a documentary, *A Hard Day's Night* (1964) is a very stylish and inventive look at The Beatles in which Richard Lester uses a simulation of the documentary approach. Other films which mimic the documentary style include a fascinating look at movie-making, *Day For Night* (1971), the police investigative thriller *He Walked By Night* (1948), and a young woman's discovery of Nazi sympathizers in her small town, the highly recommended *The Nasty Girl* (1990).

The concept of direct cinema was recently parodied in the somewhat amusing, but shocking and very violent French film, *Man Bites Dog* (1993). The film fictionalizes the making of a documentary: In attempting to film a serial murderer, the filmmakers not only fail to intervene, but become progressively more involved in manipulating the filmed scenes even to the extent of helping with the murders! This clever satire pokes fun at how easily filmmakers can get too involved in the action, reminding us that there is no clear boundary between the real and the staged. The Lumière brothers started a tradition that has become not only informative, but blurs the edges between real and pretend, upsetting our philosophical certainties.

Altered Reality

Famed director Josef von Sternberg said, "Every film is fiction because it is contrived." The idea that a documentary should have a propagandistic or subjective point of view is widespread among filmmakers and can be traced back to the Russian Dziga Vertov whose idea that "Art is not a mirror which reflects the historical struggle, but a weapon of that struggle," became an inspiration. Vertov made some amazing and challenging films including *The Man with the Movie Camera* (1929).

One of history's most influential directors was Russian Sergei Eisenstein who is esteemed for his creative use of montage (images edited together in rapid succession) and for his magnificent historical films that seem almost like documentaries, but actually take liberties with facts. His most acclaimed works are *Battleship Potemkin* (1925), with the famous Odessa steps montage, *October* (or *Ten Days That Shook the World*, 1928) which depicts the Russian revolution, and his first film, *Strike* (1924). Eisenstein spent years writing and teaching and made only a few sound films including *Alexander Nevsky* (1938) and *Ivan the Terrible* (Part I, 1945 and Part II, 1958).

British film producer John Grierson coined the term documentary and defined it as "the creative treatment of actuality." One of the earliest nonfiction films to receive both critical acclaim and widespread popularity was *Nanook of the North* (1922). In an attempt to communicate his vision, director Robert Flaherty had Eskimos wear old-fashioned clothing and reenact out-dated rituals. Similarly, In *Man of Aran* (1934), which chronicles life on the small islands near Ireland, Flaherty taught the islanders how to harpoon sharks because, as he said, "One often has to distort a thing to catch its true spirit. Sometimes you have to lie." A documentary is never completely objective. This is just as it should be according to German director Werner Herzog who claims that art must be stylized and imaginative in order to capture the real truth.

Some recent films have generated new interest in the issue of just what is the boundary between fiction and documentary. In *Roger and Me* (1989) Michael Moore stars in his satire of General Motors Corporation and freely manipulates the chronology of events. *The Thin Blue Line* (1988) argues that a convicted cop killer is innocent by using direct camera interviews (a technique parodied in 1969 by Woody Allen in the very funny film, *Take the Money and Run*). The historical epic *Reds* (1981) uses actual witnesses sprinkled throughout the film. This fictionalized drama generated extreme controversy, typified by Trevor Griffiths' comment, "History to Hollywood is a blank check." *Heavenly Creatures* (1994) fictionalizes an account of two young women (one of whom is still alive—which raises some interesting questions about the intrusiveness of films) who killed one of their mothers, and *Baby Fever* (1995), Henry Jaglom's new film, uses a quasi-documentary style to highlight modern women's concerns about having a baby. *Little Dieter Needs to Fly* (1997) by Herzog has been called the best film yet on the Vietnam War.

Neorealism

The realist concept was purposely altered in Italy just after World War II by a number of filmmakers who used movies to subjectively portray the personal, everyday lives of ordinary people. Roberto Rossellini's film *Open City* (1945) was the most influential of this Neorealist movement and his statement "This is the way things are" became its motto. *Paisan* (1946) is considered his greatest film, and his assistant, Federico Fellini went on to greatness with such films as *La Strada* (1954), *Nights of Cabiria* (1957), *La Dolce Vita* (1960), and *8 1/2* (1963). The Neorealist films are imbued with a moral, heavily emotional and compassionate eye for social truth and justice. The first of this style was *Ossessione* (1942), which was based on the James M. Cain novel *The Postman Always Rings Twice*. Because of copyright problems, the film was not seen in the U.S. for over thirty years. The Production Code Administration prevented filming of the novel until 1946 (censorship has had a major influence on films both in the U.S. and abroad for many years). The American movie version of the novel (same title) became even more popular and influential than its Italian counterpart.

The best-known Neorealist film is Vittorio De Sica's *The Bicycle Thief* (1948), which incessantly portrays the human consequences of unemployment, frustration, and pathos. For a double feature, add the 1989 satirical send-up *The Icicle Thief,* which lampoons television and artfully blends realism with absurd fantasy, or *We All Loved Each Other So Much* (1974), a tribute to the genre and dedicated to De Sica who died that year.

Several new Iranian directors have adopted the Neorealist style and given it a contemporary, philosophical feel. Some of these wonderfully quiet and contemplative films include *The White Balloon* (1996), *Taste of Cherry* (1997), and *The Apple* (1999).

Tales of the Ordinary

Although Neorealism represents a particular style and content, the underlying concept of moralizing about the lives of ordinary people has a long and international history. For example, Michelangelo Antonioni contributed films expressing deep alienation, loneliness, and malaise including *L'Avventura* (1960), *La Notte* (1961), *L'Eclisse* (1962), *Red Desert* (1964) and *Blow-Up* (1966).

One of history's most acclaimed directors was Jean Renoir (son of painter Pierre-Auguste Renoir) whose extensive oeuvre includes *Le Bête Humaine* (1938), a story of love, murder, and deceit, *Rules of the Game* (1939), a funny, dark parody of social structure and its underlying "rules," and *Grand Illusion* (1937), a non-violent portrait of relationships among soldiers during WWI. Renoir was disappointed when WWII broke out, believing that his film did not accomplish its purpose. Incidentally, a number of great films revolve around an anti-war theme: *Journey's End* (1930), *Attack* (1956), *Life and Nothing But* (1989), Stanley Kubrick's heart-breaking *Paths of Glory*, (1957) and *J'Accuse* (1919), which was re-made in 1938, from French pioneer Abel Gance, featuring the dead rising from their graves, are among the very best.

French director Eric Rohmer is known for his more modern and amusing morality tales such as *My Night at Maud's* (1969), *Clair's Knee* (1970), and *Chloe in the Afternoon* (1972). The films of German director G. W. Pabst often lean toward bittersweet realism as in *Pandora's Box* (1929) and *Diary of a Lost Girl* (1929), which star the beguiling, sensual Louise Brooks. Similarly, *Ecstasy* (1933) portrays real-life problems of love and desire. Although popular, it became one of history's most litigated films because of brief nude shots of a scintillating Hedy

Louise Brooks in *Pandora's Box*

Lamarr and the stirring depiction of her face during orgasm. Other films dramatizing the particular concerns and experiences of ordinary women include Diane Kurys' *Peppermint Soda* (1979) and *Entre Nous* (1983).

A soft, mysterious and impressionistic image from *Ugetsu*

From Japan, Yasujiro Ozu's films such as *Tokyo Story* (1953), *Equinox Flower* (1958), and *Floating Weeds* (1959) movingly depict real people, their concerns and relationships. Fellow Japanese director Kenji Mizoguchi made ninety films, many of them luminous, ravishing wonders such as *Ugetsu* (1953). Indian filmmaker Satyajit Ray directed films of beauty and power such as the Apu trilogy: *Pather Panchali* (1955), *Aparajito* (1956), and *The World of Apu* (1958). Some of the most moving and cinematically appealing films came from the Eastern bloc. Highly recommended are *The Loves of A Blonde* (1965), full of comedy, pathos, and understanding; *Closely Watched Trains* (1966), featuring tradition, politics, and premature ejaculation; *The Cranes Are Flying* (1957), a gorgeous, heart-rending portrait of love and duty in World War II Russia; *The Lady with the Dog* (1960), a tale of clandestine romance reminiscent of the highly recommended British film *Brief Encounter* (1946); and Wajda's *Man of Marble* (1976) and sequel *Man of Iron* (1981), powerful historical documents from Poland.

Victor Sjöström, whom historian David Shipman called "the screen's first master," wrote, directed, and often acted in such masterpieces as *Terje Vigen* (1917), *The Outlaw and His Wife* (1918), *The Phantom Carriage* (1921), and the Hollywood-made, *The Wind* (1928). Danish Director Carl Dreyer said, "Through Sjöström's work, film was let into art's promised land."

Dreyer was a master himself whose remarkable films include the haunting *Vampyr* (1932) and *The Passion of Joan of Arc* (1928), which consists primarily of close-ups of actress Renée Falconetti who is said to have suffered a nervous breakdown during the tense filming. Sjöström can be seen in his final film role as the lead in Ingmar Bergman's excellent *Wild Strawberries* (1957).

From Britain, the very contemporary films of Mike Leigh often highlight dreary, down-beat lives of fatalistic desperation but humorous and chagrined hopefulness, such as *Secrets and Lies* (1996).

Naked (1994) is difficult to watch, but an amazing document. In America, Frank Capra's films exemplified the tradition of ordinary people struggling to do right. Consider *Mr. Deeds Goes to Town* (1936), *Mr. Smith Goes to Washington* (1939), or *Meet John Doe* (1941). Other good examples are John Ford's best work, *The Grapes of Wrath* (1940), and the made-for-television award winner *Marty* (1955).

More recently, the works of independent filmmakers Jim Jarmusch and Hal Hartley are especially well-realized excursions into the lives of ordinary, albeit quirky and oddly humorous, people. Try *Stranger Than Paradise* (1984), *Down By Law* (1986), *Trust* (1990), *Night on Earth* (1992), *The Unbelievable Truth* (1990), and *Amateur* (1994). *Shadows* (1960) was an influential independent film that introduced John Cassavetes' loose, improvisational style, which he continued in a number of other interesting films. "Don't be afraid of anything," was Cassavetes' advice to aspiring filmmakers. Similarly, Spike Lee has directed a number of films (e.g., *Do the Right Thing*, 1989) exhibiting a stylish look at **social realism**, films that explore relationships and racial themes.

Tales of the Extraordinary

The idea that movies should reflect or portray reality is right at home with much of the movie-going public. Perhaps the most common complaint made about a movie is that it is not realistic enough. But other film fans don't agree; they want the cinema to explore the world of imagination and the unreal. To them, a realistic film is humdrum and unsatisfying; they want cinema to show what can't be seen in real life. This sentiment is not a new one.

An early fan of the Lumière's technology was the French magician, Georges Méliès who ran the Robert-Houdin theatre (named after the great magician) in Paris. When Méliès began experimenting with film, the result was a distinctly different style from what the Lumière brothers had fathomed—*cinema fantastique*!

Méliès saw that film could do much more than just record everyday events and he at once began creating films filled with magic. One day his film stuck inside the camera and after developing it he serendipitously discovered a carriage cinematically turned into a hearse! He immediately recognized the value of such camera tricks and consequently began to explore special effects. His use of trick photography, staged settings, superimpositions, fading, dissolves, slow and fast motion, miniatures, and particularly, fictional, often fantastic, stories revolutionized the making of films.

Today Méliès is recognized as the originator of the film aesthetic referred to as Formalism or Expressionism. Instead of showing us what is real, the idea is to manipulate the form of the film images in order to show something unreal, even absurd or outrageous. Méliès used film to advance the world of imagination and artistic expression. Of his five hundred some films, his most celebrated was *A Trip to the Moon* (1902), which stands as a monumental achievement in aesthetic artistry.

Fantastic Films and Expressionism

Beauty and the Beast

The Blood of a Poet

The robot woman is created in *Metropolis*

The works of Jean Cocteau, history's greatest poetic filmmaker, are excellent examples of how film can be fantastic and even lyrical in telling a story. His dreamy version of *Beauty and the Beast* (1946) well epitomizes the qualities of *cinema fantastique*. Many of Cocteau's other films are intensely personal and symbolic, particularly the trio *The Blood of a Poet* (1930), *Orpheus* (1949), and *Testament of Orpheus* (1959).

Using light and shadow to symbolize fantasy was a major theme of German Expressionism from about 1919 to 1930. Perhaps director Fritz Lang's early work is the most celebrated: The Nibelungen legend is depicted in two parts, *Siegfried* and *Kriemhild's Revenge* (1924), two of history's most impressive films because of their epic motifs, high quality cinematic values such as **mise-en-scene** (the arrangements of characters and objects in the frame), and the realization of dramatic elements; *Metropolis* (1926) presents a stunning expressionistic future world where objects and scenes penetrate below the surface to the essence of symbolism, and featuring the first robot woman created by a mad scientist; and *M* (1930), starring Peter Lorre in his first film role as a child murderer hunted by police and criminals alike.

The most influential early expressionist film was *The Cabinet of Dr. Caligari* (1919). Its striking, abstract sets evoke emotions better than any dialogue. Similar images can be seen in *The Golem* (1920), which recounts the Czech folk tale of a clay figure who comes to life to save the Jews of Prague. F. W. Murnau's dramatic, brooding *Faust* (1926) and the stylized *The Last Laugh* (1924) are among the best of the German silent era.

Siegfried rides off to find his true love

Filmed in crisp black and white, Woody Allen's *Shadows and Fog* (1992) is a tribute to German Expressionism and also reflects the paranoid mood evoked by the writings of Prague philosopher and literary stylemaster, Franz Kafka.

Czech filmmakers have produced some of the best animated and fantastic films. For example, Karel Zeman's *Baron Munchausen* (1962) mixes live actors with trick sets, very much in the style of Méliès.

Kriemhild lives to avenge Siegfried's murder

The expressionist style is also vividly realized in *Ashes and Diamonds* (1958), the finale of a trilogy exploring events in Poland at the end of World War II. The film catapulted

The face of the clay Golem

filmmaker Andrjez Wajda to international fame. His use of deep focus photography was the most effective since Orson Welles' *Citizen Kane* (1941).

Recent films reflecting the expressionist style are the zealously bureaucratic futuristic world of *Brazil* (1985); the ultra-bizarre, violent fantasy from Japan, *Iron Man* (1993); the dreamy, nebulous, often humorous atmospheres of *The City of Lost Children* (1995) and *Delicatessen* (1991) from French directors Caro and Jeunet, and the similarly styled German film, *Tuvalu (1999)*.

Surrealism and Suspense

One of the most startling approaches to Expressionism was the intellectual philosophy known as Surrealism that attempted to undo the rational world and use art to reveal the pure unconscious mind. Its goal was to expose the unsullied truth of human phenomenology by providing a raw glimpse into a mental world uncluttered by conscious or cultural censorship.

One of the first films to convey the surrealist attitude was René Clair's *The Crazy Ray* (1924), an image-laden sci-fi concoction. G. W. Pabst provided the first film based on Freud's concept of dream interpretation, *Secrets of a Soul* (1926). But it was in 1929 when Luis Buñuel and Salvador Dali unsettled the film community with *Un Chien Andalou* (*An Andalusian Dog*), a disturbing, meandering potpourri of irrational, symbolic episodes without plot. Buñuel's later work *L'Age D'Or* (1930) parodied society, religion, and capitalism and hence was received with maniacal protests including bombs thrown at the screen. His oeuvre includes some of the best surrealist movies, in fact, some of history's best movies period!

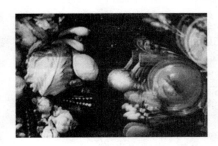

The surreal, animated images of Jan Svankmajer in *Dimensions of Dialogue*

Pure surrealist artists in the cinema are rare and not commercially successful. Perhaps the most interesting is Czech director Jan Svankmajer who calls himself a "militant surrealist." His films were banned by the Communists who once controlled Czechoslovakia on the grounds that they promoted anticommunist sentiments. His works, such as *Alice* (1988), *Faust* (1994), and *Conspirators of Pleasure* (1996) include animation as well as live action. Look for his short films including *Dimensions of Dialogue* (1982) or the documentary *The Animator of Prague* (1998) at your video store.

Two American filmmakers, the Brothers Quay (Stephen and Timothy), are devotees of Svankmajer and now live in London where they create some unique and dark animated films based on the surrealist doctrine. Their short films are available on video, including the masterful *Street of Crocodiles* (1986) inspired by the short story by Polish author Bruno Schulz, and they have recently completed an interesting live action feature film, *Institute Benjamenta* (1995).

The surrealist doctrine seeped into other films such as

Godard's *Weekend* (1968), a wicked social satire packed with images and ideas, *Peppermint Frappe* (1968), which is dedicated to Buñuel, and even into some commercial movies such as *Spellbound* (1945) directed by Alfred Hitchcock, who was not only a master filmmaker, but was willing to experiment. He was one of the first to try 3-D, in *Dial M for Murder* (1956), although the technique was too cumbersome and the film was released in normal format. In *Rope* (1948) Hitchcock used extremely limited editing, *North By Northwest* (1959) proved that suspense can be attained even in the wide-open outdoors, and in *Rear Window* (1954) Hitchcock successfully intercut extreme long shots with claustrophobic indoor shots. *Lifeboat* (1944) is a total film exercise in claustrophobia with the interesting question of how Hitchcock could make his usual cameo appearance in a film that takes place entirely in a cramped lifeboat (see it to find out!). Perhaps *Vertigo* (1958) is his best and most complex thriller, with inexorably mounting intrigue, but *Saboteur* (1942) is a fun-filled grab bag of nearly every suspense gimmick in the book, and an even better example of why Hitchcock is called the master of suspense.

The B-movie master of psychological suspense had to be producer Val Lewton. His films were inexpensive and formulaic with sleazy titles, but he got more out of less than did any other producer. There is a quiet beauty and marvelous cinematic quality to his films such as *Cat People* (1942), *The Curse of the Cat People* (1944), *I Walked with a Zombie* (1943), *The Leopard Man* (1943), and *The Seventh Victim* (1943). Although not big budget films, they show how cinematography, pacing, light, shadows, and artistic integrity can make film magic better than any gruesome blood and violence.

Director David Lynch started his career in this mode with the nightmarish *Eraserhead* (1977) and the impassioned *The Elephant Man* (1980), both of which glisten with cinematographic delights, textures, sounds, and surprises. Unfortunately his later films sludged further and further into the grime of Hollywood sex and violence. *Blue Velvet* (1986), however, is a remarkable piece of work with some very interesting subtexts as well as offbeat characters and good performances.

Dadaism and the Avant-Garde

Dadaism was an artistic philosophy that emphasized anarchy, absurdity, and the mocking of society and its conventions. In 1923 artist/photographer Man Ray was asked to make a film for a Dada gathering. He randomly pieced together bits of film he had exposed with various objects and shapes sprinkled on the raw filmstock. The result,

Charlie Chaplin parodies our
Modern Times

Return to Reason, was presented at one of the last Dada soirees and produced a near riot. In Dada-land, this was considered a great success!

Perhaps the most clever Dada film is René Clair's *Entr'acte* (1924). Created to be shown between acts of a ballet (hence the title), the short film's central focus is a funeral procession gone absurdly awry. Clair evolved well beyond Dada and became one of history's greatest filmmakers emphasizing poetic, rhythmic, visual themes accompanied by a wide range of cinematic methods. His *A Nous la Liberte* (1931) is a creative classic and influenced Charlie Chaplin's *Modern Times* (1936). Dada absurdities can also be found in the comedies of Buster Keaton, the Marx Brothers, and Monty Python, in the classic horror parody *Night of the Living Dead* (1965) and in Stanley Kubrick's brilliant anti-war farce *Dr. Strangelove* (1964).

Avant-garde and experimental filmmakers often ignored the story altogether and manipulated film in order to demonstrate pure formalist qualities. The work of German abstract painter Hans Richter is probably best known and most influential. His "absolute films" rejected narrative and sometimes consisted merely of abstract shapes and designs. Richter was one of the leaders of both Surrealism and Dada and produced some of the most creative films emphasizing form over content. Like all great artists, he used the medium to seek the underlying "truths" of reality. Film historian Arthur Knight wrote about *Rhythm 21* (1921): "Richter was concerned with texture and light, with movement drawn from inanimate things, with rhythms created by cutting." *Dreams That Money Can Buy* (1944) became Richter's best-known film, although his earlier films were pristine inspiration for the experimental film movement.

The first important American experimental film was *Life and*

Death of 9413, A Hollywood Extra (1928), influenced by German Expressionism. Dancer Maya Deren led the post World War II avant-garde filmmakers. Her *Meshes of the Afternoon* (1943), a dreamy, sur-real, personal, and sublimely poetic excursion into semiotics, became the standard bearer of experimental films. Stanley Brakhage had the most success. His *Mothlight* (1963), *Dog Star Man* (1964), and *The Act of Seeing With One's Own Eyes* (1971) are classics of the avant-garde. Other noteworthy contributors include Shirley Clarke (*The Connection*, 1961), Michael Snow (*Wavelength*, 1967), Jonas Mekas, founder and editor of *Film Culture* magazine that is devoted to essays about experi-mental films (*Brig*, 1964), Kenneth Anger (*Scorpio Rising*, 1963), James Broughton (*The Pleasure Garden*, 1954), Scott Bartlett, whose films feature electronic techniques (*Moon*, 1969), and the father of the music video, Bruce Conner (*A Movie*, 1958). Pop artist Andy Warhol and his followers (called "Hangers-On") produced many experimental films exhibiting a diverse range of styles.

Crossing Over

An experimentalist whose movies are now commercially rec-ognized is Chantal Akerman. Her work is personal, gritty, existential, and moody. Try *Je Tu Il Elle* (1986), *Night and Day* (1991), or a col-lection of her short films, *Akermania* (1992). In the 1960s a group of experimental filmmakers and critics eschewed the term underground and called their movement "New American Cinema." Their enthusiasm spread to portions of the general public and consequently film literacy and interest grew, manifested by the sprouting of film societies and art-house theaters. The first film society, Cinema 16, was organized by crit-ic Amos Vogel whose book *Film As A Subversive Art* (1974) is an aston-ishing compilation of films, photos, and analysis.

Today a new classification of films has emerged, called "cross-overs," that are both artistic enough to play the societies and art-houses yet commercial enough for the malls. The best cross-over is *The Piano* (1994), the third of Jane Campion's personal, sensitive films (a collec-tion of her short films is also available on video). Also recommended are *High Heels* (1991), *Europa Europa* (1991), *The Madness of King George* (1995), *Zentropa* (1991), the box-office smashes, *Like Water for Chocolate* (1992) and *Il Postino* (1995), the amusing and touching tale of a blind photographer, *Proof* (1991), *Run Lola Run* (1998), and *Blue* (1993), *White* (1994), and *Red* (1994), the ambitious trilogy from Krysztof Kieslowski.

Beautiful Blends

The vast number of films made today fall between the two extremes of realism and expressionism and are referred to as "classic cinema." In fact, the two different approaches are not so objectively distinct as one might at first conclude. Fellini concurred that the boundary is blurry stating: "I see no dividing line between imagination and reality."

An angel listens to a woman's inner desires in *Wings of Desire*

A good example is Wim Wenders' beautiful, mesmerizing *Wings of Desire* (1987), which uses a fantastic gimmick to portray the reality of our inner thoughts and desires: Angels listen to our private musings and yearn to join us in our mortal lives of sentience. The listening-in sequences are some of the most transcendent and introspective ever filmed. The concept is continued in the sequel, *Far Away, So Close* (1994), which unfortunately falls short because it succumbs to simplistic Hollywood-style plotting and excesses.

Since the experience of viewing a film is psychological, that is, subjective, one's interpretations, moods, and attitudes also help define the experience. Cinematic moments can be interpreted as either real or fantasy. The films of Alain Resnais and Orson Welles are good examples of how both realism and expressionism can be found on screen at the same time.

Resnais' films are mood pieces that subvert time and space. It is as if he took to heart Hans Richter's statement, "The use of the time element is at the bottom of a new magic."

The short film *Night and Fog* (1955) may be called a documentary since it includes archival footage of the Auschwitz concentration camp, but Resnais intercuts the brutal death scenes with modern day images of a quiet, empty, grassy Auschwitz and overlays all images with a poetic soundtrack. *Hiroshima, mon Amour* (1959) is part love story but with expressionist sounds, images, dialogue, and deep, haunting subtexts alluding to psychological issues. The excellent script, dreamy photography, eloquent obliqueness, and poignant, meaningful themes make this one of history's best films.

The enigmatic *Last Year at Marienbad* (1961) delves even deeper into the cinematic manipulation of memory and temporal subversion, a quality also found in Dovzhenko's brilliant episodic spectacle *Earth* (1930), Chris Marker's *La Jetée* (1963), Kurosawa's *Rashomon* (1950), and even to some extent in Griffith's classic *Intolerance* (1916) because it interweaves four chronologically different stories. The massive sets and epic Babylon story of *Intolerance* were influenced by the very popular Italian epic, *Cabiria* (1914), which led the way for the making of extravaganza films.

Lovers' arms wrapped around one another, bathed in radioactive dust in *Hiroshima, mon Amour*

Orson Welles' films appear realistic because of their content, but are full of innovative expressionist elements. *Citizen Kane* (1941) bombards the viewer with daring camera angles, stirring shadows, and long shots in deep focus. *The Lady from Shanghai* (1948) features the famous shoot-out finale in a hall of mirrors (mimicked by Woody Allen in *Manhattan Murder Mystery*, 1993). The opening camera shot of *Touch of Evil* (1958) is remarkable in that it covers so much ground for so long without an edit. Welles' Shakespearean films *Macbeth* (1948) and *Othello* (1951) also exhibit a striking expressionist style.

The hall of mirrors in *The Lady from Shanghai*

Orson Welles also appeared as an actor in many films, including the memorable role of Harry Lime in *The Third Man* (1949), a moody thriller shot in Vienna and featuring zither music. The final scenes in the sewers of the city are visually striking and reflect an expressionist influence.

Orson Welles in the haunting thriller, *The Third Man*

Jean-Luc Godard is our most intellectual modern filmmaker. In his *Les Chinois* (1967) it is stated that the Lumières fathered formalist films while Méliès was the founder of realism! This amusing bit of iconoclasm reminds us that film interpretation has a subjective nature. The audience is not static. There is an organic interplay, a synergism, between film and viewer. We each bring our subjective experiences, values, personal histories, and understandings to the event. We may all gather as an audience and share the same sounds and images, but when the film ends and the credits are rolling we sit in the dark no longer together but each with our own quietly subjective reflections. As Lily Tomlin once quipped, "Just remember, we're all in this alone."

Movies vs. Films

Film certainly can be viewed as an art form in its own right. Just as with the other arts, we would expect that the artistically inclined would enthusiastically adopt this medium and pour their creative energies into exploring its methods and boundaries, and directing its unique characteristics toward the expression of an aesthetic philosophy. We would expect. Alas, in the short course of film history there has been little evidence of film being caressed as a medium of high art.

What is patently obvious is that the cinema has become an industry of commercial exploitation. Libby Gelman-Waxner, the alter ego of film critic Paul Rudnick, thinks of movies as catalogs! This tongue-in-cheek comment is dripping with truth. Product placements are only one obvious example of the retail slant of Hollywood movies that also *sell* clothes, hairstyles, values, behaviors, and beliefs. In the United States movies are particularly aimed at teenagers and children. When asked why he doesn't seek roles in Hollywood, actor John Hurt replied, "America only makes children's pictures." In 1984 Robert De Niro opined, "Movies are in major trouble. They're aiming most of the movies at children—the most mindless, uninformative and vulgar bunch of projects."

The problem reminds one of the difference between art and craft. By craft we typically are referring to technical virtuosity and skill without regard to aesthetic sensibility. Art, on the other hand, is imbued with values, purpose, message, and meaning. Of course there is good art and bad art just as there is good and bad craft. Also, there is no clear boundary between the two, they merge and intertwine. Still, the distinction is a useful one. Slavko Vorkapich wrote, "Most films are examples not of creative use of motion picture devices and techniques, but examples of their use as recording instruments and processes only. There are extremely few motion pictures that may be cited as instances of creative use of the medium, and from these only fragments and short passages may be compared to the best achievements in other arts."

The movies coming out of Hollywood are often well crafted, but are totally lacking in artistic value. David Shipman observed, "Lucas and Spielberg may be making themselves and their backers very wealthy: at the same time they are doing their medium a profound disservice." Godard's view that "There is only one solution, to turn one's back to American cinema" may have once seemed outrageous, but is becoming progressively more acceptable. When we consider the ill effects on society together with the pandering, insipid content of the trash now being projected on pint-size screens in shopping malls, it is difficult to be optimistic.

David Putnam in 1989 warned, "The medium is too powerful and important to be left solely to the tyranny of the box-office or reduced to the sum of the lowest common denominator of public taste." But certainly we cannot rely on the moguls now in power to make a difference. This point was unintentionally and ironically made by Lloyd Kaufman who urged filmmakers, "It's up to us to produce better quality movies." Here's the clincher: Kaufman is responsible for the dimwitted dud *Stuff Stephanie in the Incinerator* (1989)! One more juicy irony: Sylvester Stallone told French TV, "I don't know where the world would be without art." Good one, Sly!

Acclaimed director John Huston, referring to Stallone's movie *Rambo* (1985), exhibited the integrity that is so sorely lacking: "I wouldn't have made it even if I'd known it was going to make so many millions of dollars." Similarly, from Charlie Chaplin in 1972: "I don't think today's films stack up to mine. They have no merit." Actor Rod Steiger gives the problem a cause: "I believe to the marrow of my bones, that as far as America is concerned, the respect for the artist is about the level of respect for the waste matter of a dog last Monday in Hyde Park." In 1985 on French TV Orson Welles lamented, "I'm not bitter about Hollywood's treatment of me—but of its treatment of Griffith, von Sternberg, Buster Keaton, and a hundred others." Erich von Stroheim expressed his frustration: "When I saw how the censors mutilated my picture Greed, which I did really with my entire heart, I abandoned all my ideals to create real art."

It has been extremely difficult to get film accepted as an art medium. Whereas other arts—for example, dance, music, painting, and literature—obviously have a commercial side, we also recognize their value as serious, aesthetic fields of study and modes of human expression. Film historian Arthur Knight observed, "While books and music are often discussed as art, movies for the most part remain just movies.

There is something so casual about seeing a film. Somehow it is too entertaining, too popular to be identified with the arts."

A manifestation of this view is the lack of film literacy among the general public and the resistance to film study as a legitimate field of academic scholarship. One college student complained, "Why should I take a film course? I already know how to watch movies." Would we hear similar comments about courses on Shakespeare, Beethoven, or Picasso? *"Why should I study literature? I already know how to read a book. Why study art? I know how to look at paintings."*

Film Excellence

Despite its feeble achievements relative to other arts, the cinema has provided certain magical moments of artistic excellence. Some filmmakers have acknowledged the complexity of film and the difficulty of achieving such moments. Man Ray observed, "I've never seen a movie that didn't have at least thirty seconds of real film in it and I've never seen one that had much more."

The films of Japanese director Akira Kurosawa are universally praised by critics, still his own evaluation is more humble: "In all my films, there's three or maybe four minutes of real cinema." Woody Allen added, "I've never made a film that could remotely be considered a masterpiece. Not even remotely." Perhaps even more to the point Allen added, "The best film I ever did—*Stardust Memories*—was my least popular film. That may automatically mean it was my best film."

But moments of excellence have occurred in film. The filmmaker who has advanced cinematic art more than anyone is Ingmar Bergman. As with most things of high value and rich reward, his films require effort to understand and appreciate. Anyone schooled in film by television and Hollywood will need time to gradually wade into Bergman's world. His themes are deep, sometimes inscrutable, the moods profoundly existential.

Bergman's films often exist on a plane above the characters, plots, and dialogue, in the shadows of symbols, ideas, and feelings. *Persona* (1966) may be the most complex movie ever made, and overall probably the best. Film Professor Louis Giannetti lists some of its themes: "The relationship of the artist to audience, the futility of communication, the need to humiliate and to be humiliated, isolation and alienation, the inscrutability of the human psyche, the need for masks and deceptive poses, unconscious sexual desires, and the inability to love."

The Seventh Seal (1957) is a masterpiece of human expression, symbolism, and philosophical musing. *Cries and Whispers* (1972) moves with deliberate foreboding, deep sadness, and unspoken psychological dynamics. Its penetrating despair, loneliness, and grim mood are also found in *The Silence* (1963), part of a trilogy embracing themes of faith, meaning, and contemplation.

Persona reveals its self-reflexive motif when a character photographs us, the viewers

The Rite (1969) and *Face to Face* (1975) have some of the same futility and somber, devastating depth of emotion, as does Bergman's exploration of a resentful mother-daughter relationship, *Autumn Sonata* (1978). *Hour of the Wolf* (1968) depicts a man's descent into madness and his wife's concomitant suffering. *The Magician* (1958), *Monika* (1952), *Smiles of a Summer Night* (1955), and *Sawdust and Tinsel* (1953) are lighter and more accessible.

The search for moments of cinematic art may also be approached via an excursion through film genres. For example, film noir movies are fatalistic and shadowy with alluring *femmes fatales* and hardboiled anti-heroes. *Double Indemnity* (1944) may be the best of this type and features an interesting use of flashback and voice-over narration. *Kiss of Death* (1947) is noteworthy for the over-the-top performance by Richard Widmark as a sadistic giggling gangster who pushes a woman in a wheelchair down a flight of stairs!

Laura (1944) includes a love story, as does *The Spiral Staircase* (1946); *Mildred Pierce* (1945) reeks with bitterness, but has an oddly humorous atmosphere; *Detour* (1945) exhibits the ironic destiny common to the genre; and *The Maltese Falcon* (1941), *Murder, My Sweet* (1944), *The Big Sleep* (1946), and *Out of the Past* (1947) are often cited as classic examples of film noir. Also try *Without Pity* (1949), a thriller from Italy co-written by Fellini. The most fun is *Kiss Me Deadly* (1955), which maintains a tongue-in-cheek parody of the macho style until the incredible climax that explodes with allusions to greed, paranoia, and the atomic bomb!

Who would have guessed it, but one of the richest veins of artistic excellence can be found in the horror genre. Besides such classics as *Nosferatu* (1922), *Frankenstein* (1931), *Dracula* (1931), and *The Invisible Man* (1933), it is marvelous fun to explore the relatively more

The all-powerful robot Gort warns Earthlings to change their violent ways in *The Day the Earth Stood Still*

obscure: *Freaks* (1932) authentically and bizarrely lives up to its title; *The Old Dark House* (1932) is whimsical, off-beat fun and literally the darkest movie ever made; the best sequel, *Bride of Frankenstein* (1935) exudes wit and style, while *Young Frankenstein* (1974) is an often hilarious spoof; *Blade Runner* (1982) is a gritty and bittersweet futuristic tale with substance and integrity; *Island of Lost Souls* (1933) includes macabre de-humanizing experiments; *The Incredible Shrinking Man* (1957) maintains an effectively pensive philosophical tone; *The Day the Earth Stood Still* (1951) is arguably the best of the 1950s sci-fi films, a wonderful piece of paranoia and the inevitable human foibles, and features intellectual visitor Klaatu and his giant robot, Gort; Charles Laughton's only directed film, *Night of the Hunter* (1955), is a tense piece with exquisite cinematography; and *Carnival of Souls* (1962) shows how photography, lighting, and pacing can create a very effective mood on a very low budget!

Film artistry reached its peak in 1959-60 with the release of some phenomenal films including *Hiroshima, mon Amour, L'Avventura, Shadows, Testament of Orpheus, La Dolce Vita*, Hitchcock's *North by Northwest* and *Psycho*, Bergman's *Virgin Spring*, Robert Bresson's *Pickpocket*, and from the French New Wave, Godard's *Breathless,* and Truffaut's *The 400 Blows* and *Shoot the Piano Player*. Even Hollywood contributed *Some Like It Hot, Spartacus, The Apartment,* and *Ben Hur*. The following decade was filled with more extraordinary films culminating in the greatest science-fiction movie ever made, *2001: A Space Odyssey* (1968).

Those years were a cineaste's delight with such bounty as *Jules and Jim* (1962), a lyrical charmer, beautifully realized; Hitchcock's suspense classic *The Birds* (1963); from Godard: *Contempt* (1963) starring director Fritz Lang, *Band of Outsiders* (1964), *Pierrot le Fou* (1965), *Alphaville* (1965), and *Masculin-Feminin* (1966); Bergman's *Through a Glass Darkly* (1961) and *Shame* (1968); the epic

Lawrence of Arabia (1962) with a young Peter O'Toole in fine form; the courtroom drama, *To Kill A Mockingbird* (1962); an amazing adventure documentary exploring primitive cultures, *The Sky Above, the Mud Below* (1961); *Sundays and Cybele* (1962), a touching tale of a disturbed man's attachment to a young girl; *The Innocents* (1961), a suspense thriller based on *The Turn of the Screw*; Buñuel contributed a number of masterful pas-

A dreamy, child-like image from
The Night of the Hunter

tiches of Surrealism including *The Exterminating Angel* (1962) and *Viridiana* (1962), with the famous visual pun of da Vinci's painting, *The Last Supper*; Robert Bresson gave us an austere *The Trial of Joan of Arc* (1962), the touching tale of a teen-age girl, *Mouchette* (1966), and a sensitive **allegory** about the life cycle of a donkey, *Au Hasard Balthazar* (1966); *Repulsion* (1965), a stylized, expressionist depiction of a woman's mental collapse; Orson Welles' Shakespearean rendering, *Chimes at Midnight* (1967); and many others that provided moments of artistic excellence in abundance—an unsurpassed decade of film.

Finally

How then should we judge cinema's one hundred years? If our standard is the morass of recent Hollywood movies, then, to paraphrase Edison, it wasn't worth it. In fact, when considering the juvenile, trashy and exploitative, pandering nature of the vast majority of movies produced today, then Lumière may have had a valid point: they may ruin you—in spirit and humanity anyway.

But if we look to the edges and rims of the art, if we scour and comb, then some treasures of artistic integrity and cinematic magic can be uncovered and savored. In those special moments, film may deservedly be called the art of the twentieth century.

Appendix A

MILESTONES IN
FILM HISTORY

1839   Development of photography
1864   First color photographs made
1870s   Celluloid, a synthetic plastic is invented, later to be used for
        filmstock; Eadweard Muybridge experiments with sequential photography
1877   Thomas Edison patents phonograph
1885   George Eastman invents film
1887   Eadweard Muybridge publishes his sequential photographs in
        The Human Figure in Motion
1888   George Eastman invents Kodak box camera with roll of film
        inside
1889   Celluloid is used as base for film
1890   Edison's employee William Dickson develops sprocket holes
        for advancing film and constructs a camera and a viewing
        machine, the Kinetoscope
1894   Marconi builds first radio; the first Kinetoscope parlor is
        opened
1895   Lumière brothers invent the Cinematographe and show the
        first projected films on screen on December 28
1896   First films projected on screen in U.S. on April 23
1902   Georges Méliès makes *A Trip to the Moon*
1903   Wright brothers first flight in airplane; Edwin Porter releases
        The Great Train Robbery

1905-   Experiments with editing lead to a classical continuity editing
1910   style that is still used today

1910-   Slapstick comedy films became popular, including those of
1930s   Charlie Chaplin (the world's first movie star), Buster
        Keaton, and the Keystone Kops (Mack Sennett)

1914   Italian epic *Cabiria* influences filmmaking
1915   Griffith's *The Birth of a Nation*
1916   Griffith's *Intolerance* introduces thematic montage

1917	The UFA studio is formed in Germany and begins producing many influential films
1919	*The Cabinet of Dr. Caligari* becomes the most influential German Expressionist film
1920s	Radio broadcasting begins; film theaters built around the world; avant-garde films begin; animated films begin; Russian Lev Kuleshov discovers the "Kuleshov effect," showing that shots are interpreted based on surrounding shots
1922	*Nosferatu; Nanook of the North*
1924	*Greed; The Last Laugh; Die Nibelungen (Siegfried and Kriemhild's Revenge)*
1925	Eisenstein's *Battleship Potemkin* influences the editing technique known as montage
1926	Fritz Lang's *Metropolis*; Hitchcock's first film *The Lodger*; John Grierson coins the term "documentary"
1927	Abel Gance's film *Napoleon* uses three projectors to create a widescreen effect
1928	First TV broadcast
1929	*The Man with the Movie Camera* (Dziga Vertov) illustrates *Kino Pravda* (cinema vérité)
1931	Fritz Lang's first sound film, the sociological murder drama, *M*
1934	The Hollywood Production Code is introduced in order to regulate film content
1935	The Nazi propaganda film *Triumph of the Will*; Hitchcock's *The 39 Steps*
1937	Renoir's *Grand Illusion*
1939	Renoir's *Rules of the Game*; many Hollywood favorites including *The Wizard of Oz* and *Gone with the Wind*
1930s–1940s	Popular and influential films by John Ford and Frank Capra; horror films influenced by German Expressionism; popular genres screwball comedies and musicals
1941	Orson Welles' *Citizen Kane*; Henri Chretien develops the anamorphic lens
1943	Hollywood's most popular movie, *Casablanca*; Maya Deren's influential poetic experimental film, *Meshes of the Afternoon*
1945	Italian Neorealism begins with Rossellini's *Open City*; Eisenstein's *Ivan the Terrible*

1940s	Numerous film noir movies from Hollywood including *The Maltese Falcon* (1941) and *Double Indemnity* (1944)
1946	U.S. TV networks begin broadcasting
1947	HUAC hearings on Hollywood begin era of Communism scare and blacklisting
1948	*The Bicycle Thief* defines the Italian Neorealist style
1950s	Widescreen; 3-D movies; new color film processes; science fiction genre films
1950	Kurosawa's *Rashomon*
1954	Kurosawa's *The Seven Samurai*; Fellini's *La Strada*
1957	Bergman's *The Seventh Seal* and *Wild Strawberries*
1958	Andrzej Wajda's *Ashes and Diamonds*
1959	French New Wave films *Breathless, The 400 Blows*, and *Hiroshima, mon Amour*
1960	Hitchcock's *Psycho*; Antonioni's *L'Avventura*; experimental film *Shadows* by John Cassavetes
1960s–1970s	Golden era of American films including *Bonnie & Clyde, The Graduate, Annie Hall, Midnight Cowboy, Nashville, Network*, and *The Godfather*
1964	Experimental filmmaker Stanley Brakhage's *Dog Star Man*
1968	Kubrick's *2001: A Space Odyssey* reshapes the sci-fi genre; the Hollywood Code is replaced by the Ratings System
1970	*The Sorrow and the Pity*, four-hour long documentary about Nazi occupation of France, by Marcel Ophuls
1977	*Star Wars* defines the mega-blockbuster with tie-ins to toys and fast-food
1980	*The Elephant Man* and *Raging Bull* maintain black and white film artistry
1984	Chen Kaige's *Yellow Earth* puts Chinese films on the map
1985	The holocaust film, *Shoah*, is over nine hours long
1987	*Wings of Desire* by Wim Wenders
1990s	American directors Spike Lee, Oliver Stone, Errol Morris, Jim Jarmusch, and Hal Hartley; beginning of digital movies; Iranian directors renew the Neorealist style; Kieslowski
1995	Dogma 95 by artistic Danish directors
2000	Continued influence of digital videos; *Time Code*; Hollywood action blockbusters dominate worldwide; artistic films from Eastern Europe, Iran, Asia, Latin and South America, and Scandinavia

Appendix B

ART MOVEMENTS &
REPRESENTATIVE FILMS

*D*uring the twentieth century, Modern and Post-Modern artistic sensibilities gave rise to many diverse movements in art, literature, and philosophy. What follows is a list of some of the most influential of these movements presented chronologically, a brief description of each, and an attempt to classify a number of films within each movement on the basis of the fundamental nature of their form and style of expression. This is a somewhat difficult task since most films follow a conventional style (a blend of many art movements), films have their own movements that do not cross over into art in general (e.g., film noir), and we may disagree about the fundamental design and style of a particular film because of its ambiguity and the variety of styles it uses. However, it may be helpful to attempt to place the cinema within the stream of artistic movements of the past century.

Realism

Gustave Courbet in 1861 wrote, "The art of painting should consist solely of the representation of objects visible and tangible to the artist." Realism was, and continues to be, a popular and influential movement, but its original intent was far beyond the literal look of a representation. The Realists believed that the subjects of art should be the common, ordinary, everyday events of life. They rejected the notion that art should deal with abstract, imaginary, or fictitious subjects.

Representative Films: Most modern films have a high degree ofRealism in their look, although only a small number deal with everyday people and events. The Italian Neorealist films, such as *The Bicycle Thief* (1948), certainly fit this category. American director John Ford had a strong realist bent to his films. Even more so, new Iranian films such as *Taste of Cherry* (1997) express a deep Neorealist style. Also, the films of Mike Leigh, such as *Secrets and Lies* (1996), and Ken Loach

(*Kes*, 1969 and *Raining Stones*, 1993) are in the realist tradition. Most nonfiction films fit here, particularly cinema vérité, such as *Salesman* (1969), and some documentaries, for example, *Brother's Keeper* (1992).

Impressionism

This very popular and influential movement was a reaction against Realism. It began with painting and later emerged in music. The term was first used in 1874 and was derived from a painting by Claude Monet titled *Impression: Sunrise*. Monet and Edouard Manet were the leading artists in this style. Monet's paintings look as if they are bathed in light. Impressionists attempted to record objects based on the transient effects of light and color on their surfaces. They used natural light and sunny conditions, for example, often rendering the play of light upon water. Landscapes were common subjects and short, choppy brush strokes gave the paintings a fuzzy, atmospheric look. Up close, these works often appeared to be just blotches of colors, but at a distance recognizable subjects emerged. The color splotches took on form and meaning.

Representative Films: A group of French filmmakers during the 1920s were known as Impressionists, but their films did not emphasize the impressionist look so much as they focused on inner mental states and psychological issues. The leader of the group was author Louis Delluc and on the fringes was the great master Abel Gance whose films *J'Accuse* (1919 & 1938) and *Napoleon* (1927) were very influential. Jean Vigo's *L'Atalante* (1934) is close to this movement, as are the films of French auteur Jean Renoir, such as *Grand Illusion* (1937) and *Rules of the Game* (1939), though Renoir is more appropriately dubbed a Poetic Realist. Films that have an impressionist look or feel to them include *Sunrise* (1927), *Pandora's Box* (1928), *Shanghai Express* (1932), *Ecstasy* (1933), *These Three* (1936), *Of Mice and Men* (1939), *Rebecca* (1940), *Laura* (1944), *Brief Encounter* (1946), *Portrait of Jennie* (1949), *They Live By Night* (1949), *Ugetsu* (1953), *Lust for Life* (1956), *The Incredible Shrinking Man* (1957), *Jules and Jim* (1962), *Lawrence of Arabia* (1962), *Woman in the Dunes* (1964), *In Cold Blood* (1967), *Manhattan* (1979), and *Altered States* (1980).

Symbolism

This far-reaching and influential literary and artistic movement was originated in 1886 by poet Jean Moreas whose manifesto proclaimed that art should "Clothe the idea in a sensitive form." This meant that art and literature should seek not to describe nature and the real world, but that art should express ideas through symbols. Much, if not all, of Modernist art and literature is based on symbolism, though this movement aimed at a higher, more poetic sensibility than just the use of signs that refer to something else.

Representative Films: Jean Cocteau was perhaps the greatest poet filmmaker and his symbolist works include *The Blood of a Poet* (1930) and *Orpheus* (1949). Maya Deren's experimental films also were symbolic and poetic, including *Meshes of the Afternoon* (1943). The films of Stan Brakhage such as *Dog Star Man* (1964) also fall within this concept, as do many of the films of Peter Greenaway such as *Drowning by Numbers* (1988). Other symbolic or poetic works include *The Wind* (1928), *The Day the Earth Stood Still* (1951), *Rear Window* (1954), *Night and Fog* (1955), *Forbidden Planet* (1956), *The Seventh Seal* (1957), *Hiroshima, mon Amour* (1959), *Shadows* (1959), *Lawrence of Arabia* (1962), *La Jetée* (1963), *The Birds* (1963), *Contempt* (1963), *Chimes at Midnight* (1967), *2001: A Space Odyssey* (1968), *Spirit of the Beehive* (1973), *Apocalypse Now* (1979), *Koyaanisqatsi* (1983), *Man Facing Southeast* (1986), *Babette's Feast* (1987), *Tampopo* (1987), *Barton Fink* (1991), *The Piano* (1993), *Caro Diario* (1994), *Underground* (1995), *Il Postino* (1995), and *Little Dieter Needs to Fly* (1997).

Fauuism

This movement had no manifestos or philosophies, but was a generic term for the use of vivid, incongruous colors in paintings and the depiction of primitive subjects. The term literally means "wild beasts," and was coined by a critic who was criticizing paintings by Henri Matisse and others at a Paris exhibit in 1905. Fauve paintings make use of aggressive execution and unnatural colors, for example, a person with a bright green face. Fauves also use primitive painting styles that look unsophisticated and rough.

Representative Films: Unfortunately, there are no films in the extreme Fauvist style, for example, using incongruous colors. However, some films approach a "wild beast" attitude in their audacity and boldness. *Yellow Submarine* (1968), *Ju Dou* (1987), *High Heels* (1990), *Prospero's Books* (1991), *The Lovers on the Bridge* (1991), and *The Pillow Book* (1997) come to mind in this regard.

Cubism

Coined in 1908 by an art critic complaining about the paintings of Georges Braque, this became one of Modern art's most influential movements. Cubist art attempted to remove objects from a fixed time and space, and instead tried to show multiple perspectives at once. One can see in a Cubist painting of a face, for example, a side perspective and a front view at the same time. The works were fragmented, stylized, and full of geometric shapes, hence the name. Braque and Pablo Picasso were the chief cubist artists; some say *Demoiselles d'Avignon* of 1907 by Picasso was the first Cubist work. In 1912 Marcel Duchamp contributed the very influential *Nude Descending a Staircase* (see page 93).

Representative Films: Ingmar Bergman's *Persona* (1966) is likely the cinema's most pure example of the attempt to show multiple sides of personality. *Time Code* (2000) is the best example of a Cubist approach to story and characters since we see four perspectives at once. Other films that try to show various perspectives are *Rashomon* (1950), *Repulsion* (1965), *Blow-Up* (1966), *Little Big Man* (1970), *Apocalypse Now* (1979), *sex, lies, & videotape* (1989), *Living in Oblivion* (1995), *Flirt* (1996), *Zentropa* (1991), *Winter Sleepers* (1997), and *Run Lola Run* (1998).

Futurism

This movement was founded by Italian author F. T. Marinetti in a 1909 manifesto that was later embraced by a wide range of artists from painting, literature, music, and architecture. Additional manifestos were written by other artists who argued for a break from Classical foundations of art in favor of motifs of movement, speed, and dynamism that were in synch with the Industrial Revolution. Futurism was particularly popular in Russia. The artists stated a commitment to social justice, the movement was allied with Cubism and Dada, and it was the first art movement to incorporate modern industrial techniques.

Representative Films: The early Russian films of Pudovkin, Eisenstein, Vertov, Dovzhenko, and others are often said to be associated with this movement. These include *Strike* (1924), *Battleship Potemkin* (1925), *Mother* (1926), *October* (1928), *Arsenal* (1929), *The Man with the Movie Camera* (1929), *Earth* (1930), and *Ivan the Terrible* (1945 & 1958). In addition, industrial themes can be found in *Ballet Mecanique* (1924), *Metropolis* (1926), *Frankenstein* (1931), *Things to Come* (1936), and even in recent films such as *The Terminator* (1984), *Brazil* (1985), *Pi* (1998), and *Tuvalu* (1999).

Expressionism

Coined in 1911, the term refers to a style of art in which the focus is on the expression of the artist's feelings and ideas instead of on representing objects. Expressionism was essentially a reaction against Impressionism. Originally associated with Germany, the movement later spread to many societies and encompassed an abstract, free-flowing design. The idea was for the artist to express inner feelings, zeal, and emotion, turning away from nature and toward the human spirit. Large color areas and dramatic brushstrokes were common. Van Gogh paved the way for Expressionism, which was later taken up by a group of New York artists, such as de Kooning, Rothko, and Pollock, known as Abstract Expressionists.

Representative Films: Best examples are the German films of the 1920s such as *The Cabinet of Dr. Caligari* (1919), *The Golem* (1920), *Nosferatu* (1922), *Faust* (1926), and *Metropolis* (1926). Many films of the 1920s and 1930s were influenced by this style including *The*

Phantom of the Opera (1925), 1931's *Frankenstein* and *Dracula*, 1932's *Freaks*, *The Mummy*, and *Vampyr*, *Island of Lost Souls* (1933), and 1939's *Wuthering Heights* and *The Hunchback of Notre Dame*. Film noir also was influenced, including *Double Indemnity* (1944), *Out of the Past* (1946), *The Lady from Shanghai* (1948), and *Touch of Evil* (1958). More recent films showing a good deal of Expressionism include *Eraserhead* (1977), *The Elephant Man* (1980), *Zelig* (1983), *Shadows and Fog* (1992), *Brazil* (1985), *Delicatessen* (1991), *The City of Lost Children* (1995), *Batman* (1989), *Pi* (1998) and *Tuvalu* (1999).

Suprematism

Invented by Kasimir Malevich and described in his book *The Non-Objective World*, this brief movement was based on abandoning natural objects in favor of "new symbols with which to render direct feelings." Malevich posited that a Suprematist "does not observe and does not touch—he feels." The new symbols the artists used at first were triangles, squares, and circles. A 1915 exhibit showed paintings of simple geometric compositions. Later, more complex shapes were used and this movement had a good deal of influence on graphic design.

Representative Films: The early short film *Ballet Mecanique* (1924) makes good use of geometric shapes and the films of Fritz Lang often have an architectural style. *Kriemhild's Revenge* (1924), for example, is loaded with geometric shapes. *Last Year at Marienbad* (1961) similarly uses mise-en-scene in an overtly geometric way.

Dadaism

Founded by Hugo Ball in Zurich in 1916, this group of artists was reacting against the tragedies of WWI and argued that if the horrors of war came from rational thinking, then it was time to try irrationality! In that vein, the name Dada was selected because it is a nonsense word. Their manifesto said it was time to draw attention to "the few independent spirits who live for their ideals." Dada leaned toward nihilistic anti-art, but produced some of the most remarkably creative and innovative works. As parody, as an attack on acceptable forms of art, and as an attempt to engage a discussion about the nature of art, Marcel

Duchamp created a picture of the *Mona Lisa* with a mustache and an obscene caption. Dadaists put images together in new, striking ways and created the collage style of design. They also initiated "found art," for example Duchamp entered a signed urinal into an art exhibit.

Representative Films: *Return to Reason* (1923) by Man Ray and *Entr'acte* (1924) by René Claire are the seminal Dada films. The silliness and absurdity of Dada is evident in films by the Marx Brothers, Charlie Chaplin, Buster Keaton, and Monty Python, for example, *Our Hospitality* (1923), *Horse Feathers* (1932), *Duck Soup* (1933), *Modern Times* (1936), *Monty Python and the Holy Grail* (1975), and *Monty Python's The Meaning of Life* (1983). Other films emphasizing the absurd are *Dr. Strangelove* (1964), *Night of the Living Dead* (1965), *Eraserhead* (1977), and *Zero Effect* (1998). Irrationality can be found in some Eastern European films and South American films such as *Death of a Bureaucrat* (1966) and *The Firemen's Ball* (1967).

Surrealism

Theater, painting, literature, and even politics were influenced by this approach founded by the 1924 manifesto of French philosopher André Breton. Surrealism was based on the fundamental teaching of Sigmund Freud that the unconscious mind holds truths that need to be revealed. Surrealist artists often used their dreams to inspire their art. Salvador Dali's 1931 painting *Persistence of Memory* featuring a melting clock is a well-known example. Breton wrote, "I believe in the future resolution of these two states which in appearance are so contradictory, that of the dream, and that of reality, into a kind of absolute reality, a surreality if one may call it such." Surrealism was a reaction against rationalism, and in that sense is akin to Dada. In fact, the two eventually merged.

Representative Films: Luis Buñuel is the most acclaimed surrealist filmmaker. His early films *Un Chien Andalou* (1929) and *L'Age D'Or* (1930) are seminal works in this style. His oeuvre is long and includes *Viridiana* (1962), *The Exterminating Angel* (1967), *The Phantom of Liberty* (1974) and *That Obscure Object of Desire* (1977). Czech filmmaker Jan Svankmajer is also a major surrealist and some of his short films as well as *Alice* (1988), *Faust* (1994), and *Conspirators of Pleasure* (1996) are available on video. Other films with a Surrealist edge are *Spellbound* (1945), *The Night of the Hunter* (1955), *The Manchurian Candidate* (1962), and *Wild Strawberries* (1957). Many films from Mexico and Latin and South America also reflect the Surrealist style, such as *Like Water for Chocolate* (1992), *Man Facing Southeast* (1986), and *Recipes for Staying Together* (1997).

Existentialism

This is not a term that is used in the visual arts, but rather one that applies to a wide range of literary and philosophical works and ideas. The term is imprecise, referring more to a family of concepts within philosophy including the ideas of Martin Heidegger, Søren Kierkegaard, and Jean-Paul Sartre; and also styles of literature, including works by Albert Camus, Franz Kafka, Simone de Beauvoir, and Dostoyevsky. Existentialism deals with profound topics related to death and the meaning of life. People are not viewed as detached observers of the world, but as "in the world," having freedom and choices. The world is viewed as absurd and incomprehensible. The emphasis is on being rather than knowing. Themes include authenticity, faith, values, and the attempt to live in a world that is inexplicable. Existentialism had a wide influence on psychology, politics, and other fields.

Representative Films: The films of Ingmar Bergman, Federico Fellini, Michelangelo Antonioni, and Werner Herzog often deal with existential themes. These include *The Seventh Seal* (1957), *La Strada* (1954), *L'Avventura* (1960), *The Silence* (1963), *Winter Light* (1963), *Even Dwarfs Started Small* (1970), *Aguirre: The Wrath of God* (1972), *Cries and Whispers* (1972), and *The Mystery of Kaspar Hauser* (1974). American independent filmmaker Jim Jarmusch portrays characters struggling with issues and circumstances that convey a sense of absurdity, coincidence, and search for understanding, for example in *Stranger Than Paradise* (1984), *Mystery Train* (1989), *Night on Earth* (1991), and *Dead Man* (1996). Krzysztof Kieslowski's films often involve motifs of coincidence, fate, and human choices, as in the *Three Colors* trilogy. Other films that reflect existential themes are *Interiors* (1978), *Being There* (1979), *My Dinner with André* (1982), *Blue Velvet* (1986), *Wings of Desire* (1987), and *Mindwalk* (1990).

Appendix C

IMPORTANT AMERICAN FILMS

The Great Train Robbery (1903) by Edwin S. Porter
The Birth of a Nation (1915) by D.W. Griffith
Intolerance (1916) by D.W. Griffith
Cleopatra (1917) by J. Gordon Edwards
Stella Maris (1918) by Marshall Nellan
True Heart Susie (1919) by D.W. Griffith
Blind Husbands (1919) by Erich von Stroheim
Broken Blossoms (1919) by D.W. Griffith
Dr. Jekyll and Mr. Hyde (1920) by John S. Robertson
Tol'able David (1921) by Henry King
Nanook of the North (1922) by Robert Flaherty
Orphans of the Storm (1922) by D. W. Griffith
Robin Hood (1922) by Allan Dwan
Foolish Wives (1922) by Erich von Stroheim
Our Hospitality (1923) by Buster Keaton and Jack Blystone
The Ten Commandments (1924) by Cecil B. DeMille
Sherlock Jr. (1924) by Buster Keaton
The Thief of Bagdad (1924) by Raoul Walsh
Greed (1924) by Erich von Stroheim
The Gold Rush (1925) by Charlie Chaplin
Tumbleweeds (1925) by William S. Hart
The Phantom of the Opera (1925) by Rupert Julian
What Price Glory? (1926) by Raoul Walsh
The Jazz Singer (1927) by Alan Crosland
Wings (1927) by William Wellman
Sunrise (1927) by F.W. Murnau
Steamboat Bill Jr. (1928) by Charles F. Reisner
The Wind (1928) by Victor Seastrom (Sjöström)
The Crowd (1928) by King Vidor
All Quiet on the Western Front (1930) by Lewis Milestone
Animal Crackers (1930) by Victor Heerman
Hell's Angels (1930) by Howard Hughes
Abraham Lincoln (1930) by D.W. Griffith

The Front Page (1931) by Lewis Milestone
City Lights (1931) by Charlie Chaplin
Public Enemy (1931) by William Wellman
Dr. Jekyll and Mr. Hyde (1931) by Rouben Mamoulian
Frankenstein (1931) by James Whale
Dracula (1931) by Tod Browning
Love Me Tonight (1932) by Rouben Mamoulian
Grand Hotel (1932) by Edmund Goulding
The Mummy (1932) by Karl Freund
Movie Crazy (1932) by Clyde Bruckman
Shanghai Express (1932) by Josef von Sternberg
Scarface (1932) by Howard Hawks
Horse Feathers (1932) by Norman Z. McLeod
Freaks (1932) by Tod Browning
The Invisible Man (1933) by James Whale
King Kong (1933) by Merian C. Coopert and Ernest B. Schoedsack
Island of Lost Souls (1933) by Erle C. Kenton
Duck Soup (1933) by the Marx Brothers
Little Women (1933) by George Cukor
Mystery of the Wax Museum (1933) by Michael Curtiz
The Gold Diggers of 1933 (1933) by Mervyn LaRoy
Cleopatra (1934) by Cecil B. DeMille
The Scarlet Empress (1934) by Josef von Sternberg
It Happened One Night (1934) by Frank Capra
Babes in Toyland (1934) by Gus Meius
The Gay Divorceé (1934) by Mark Sandrich
The Man Who Knew Too Much (1934) by Alfred Hitchcock
The Thin Man (1934) by W.S. Van Dyke
Top Hat (1935) by Mark Sandrich
The Devil is a Woman (1935) by Josef von Sternberg
The 39 Steps (1935) by Alfred Hitchcock
The Informer (1935) by John Ford
The Bride of Frankenstein (1935) By James Whale
A Tale of Two Cities (1935) by Jack Conway
Mutiny on the Bounty (1935) by Frank Lloyd
42nd Street (1935) by Lloyd Bacon
Things to Come (1936) by William Cameron Menzie
Road to Glory (1936) by Howard Hawks
Modern Times (1936) by Charlie Chaplin
Sabotage (1936) by Alfred Hitchcock
Mr. Deeds Goes to Town (1936) by Frank Capra
Dracula's Daughter (1936) by Lambert Hillyer

These Three (1936) by William Wyler
Snow White and the Seven Dwarfs (1937) by Walt Disney
Way Out West (1937) by James Horne
Nothing Sacred (1937) by William Wellman
Stage Door (1937) by Gregory LaCava
Pygmalion (1938) by Anthony Asquith
Trade Winds (1938) by Tay Garnett
Bringing Up Baby (1938) by Howard Hawks
Ninotchka (1939) by Ernst Lubitsch
Stagecoach (1939) by John Ford
Gunga Din (1939) by George Stevens
Gone with the Wind (1939) by Victor Fleming
The Wizard of Oz (1939) by Victor Fleming
Mr. Smith Goes to Washington (1939) by Frank Capra
Of Mice and Men (1939) by Lewis Milestone
Young Mr. Lincoln (1939) by John Ford
The Hunchback of Notre Dame (1939) by William Dieterle
Wuthering Heights (1939) by William Wyler
Foreign Correspondent (1940) by Alfred Hitchcock
The Philadelphia Story (1940) by George Cukor
Rebecca (1940) by Alfred Hitchcock
Fantasia (1940) by Walt Disney
The Sea Hawk (1940) by Michael Curtiz
The Thief of Bagdad (1940) by Michael Powell
His Girl Friday (1940) by Howard Hawks
The Grapes of Wrath (1940) by John Ford
Here Comes Mr. Jordan (1941) by Alexander Hall
All That Money Can Buy (1941) by William Dieterle
Meet John Doe (1941) by Frank Capra
Suspicion (1941) by Alfred Hitchcock
The Lady Eve (1941) by Preston Sturges
The Maltese Falcon (1941) by John Huston
Citizen Kane (1941) by Orson Welles
How Green Was My Valley (1941) by John Ford
To Be or Not to Be (1942) by Ernst Lubitsch
Now Voyager (1942) by Irving Rapper
Saboteur (1942) by Alfred Hitchcock
Cat People (1942) by Jacques Tourneur
The Talk of the Town (1942) by George Stevens
The Magnificent Ambersons (1942) by Orson Welles
Casablanca (1942) by Michael Curtiz
Shadow of a Doubt (1943) by Alfred Hitchcock

The Miracle of Morgan's Creek (1943) by Preston Sturges
Meshes of the Afternoon (1943) by Maya Deren
The Ox Bow Incident (1943) by William Wellman
It Happened Tomorrow (1944) by René Clair
Laura (1944) by Otto Preminger
To Have and Have Not (1944) by Howard Hawks
Double Indemnity (1944) by Billy Wilder
Sullivan's Travels (1944) by Preston Sturges
Henry V (1944) by Laurence Olivier
Lifeboat (1944) by Alfred Hitchcock
Jane Eyre (1944) by Robert Stevenson
And Then There Were None (1945) by René Clair
The Lost Weekend (1945) by Billy Wilder
Detour (1945) by Edgar G. Ulmer
Scarlet Street (1945) by Fritz Lang
Spellbound (1945) by Alfred Hitchcock
It's a Wonderful Life (1946) by Frank Capra
The Best Years of Our Life (1946) by William Wyler
Gilda (1946) by Charles Vidor
My Darling Clementine (1946) by John Ford
Notorious (1946) by Alfred Hitchcock
Spiral Staircase (1946) by Robert Siodmak
The Big Sleep (1946) by Howard Hawks
Out of the Past (1947) by Jacques Tourneur
Gentleman's Agreement (1947) by Elia Kazan
Crossfire (1947) by Edward Dmytryk
The Time of Your Life (1948) by H. C. Potter
The Snake Pit (1948) by Anatole Litvak
He Walked By Night (1948) by Alfred L. Werker
The Naked City (1948) by Jules Dassin
Treasure of the Sierra Madre (1948) by John Huston
Rope (1948) by Alfred Hitchcock
Oliver Twist (1948) by David Lean
The Red Shoes (1948) by Michael Powell
Red River (1948) by Howard Hawks
Lady from Shanghai (1948) by Orson Welles
Portrait of Jennie (1949) by William Dieterle
On the Town (1949) by Gene Kelly and Stanley Donen
D. O. A. (1949) by Rudolph Mate
Adam's Rib (1949) by George Cukor
The Big Steal (1949) by Don Siegel
They Live By Night (1949) by Nicholas Ray

The Third Man (1949) by Carol Reed
Harvey (1950) by Henry Koster
All About Eve (1950) by Joseph Mankiewicz
In a Lonely Place (1950) by Nicholas Ray
Panic in the Streets (1950) by Elia Kazan
Sunset Boulevard (1950) by Billy Wilder
Strangers on a Train (1951) by Alfred Hitchcock
Paths of Glory (1951) by Stanley Kubrick
The African Queen (1951) by John Huston
The Day the Earth Stood Still (1951) by Robert Wise
A Streetcar Named Desire (1951) by Elia Kazan
Othello (1951) by Orson Welles
Singin' In the Rain (1952) by Gene Kelly and Stanley Donen
Niagara (1952) by Henry Hathaway
High Noon (1952) by Fred Zinnemann
Stalag 17 (1953) by Otto Preminger
From Here to Eternity (1953) by Fred Zinnemann
Shane (1953) by George Stevens
The Big Heat (1953) by Fritz Lang
Creature from the Black Lagoon (1954) by Jack Arnold
The Caine Mutiny (1954) by Edward Dmytryk
On the Waterfront (1954) by Elia Kazan
Rear Window (1954) by Alfred Hitchcock
Kiss Me Deadly (1955) by Robert Aldrich
Rebel Without a Cause (1955) by Nicholas Ray
Marty (1955) by Delbert Mann
The Man with the Golden Arm (1955) by Otto Preminger
The Night of the Hunter (1955) by Charles Laughton
The Searchers (1956) by John Ford
Lust for Life (1956) by Vincente Minnelli
Friendly Persuasion (1956) by William Wyler
Forbidden Planet (1956) by Fred M. Wilcox
The Ten Commandments (1956) by Cecil B. DeMille
Giant (1956) by George Stevens
Invasion of the Body Snatchers (1956) by Don Siegel
Saint Joan (1957) by Otto Preminger
The Incredible Shrinking Man (1957) by Jack Arnold
The Wrong Man (1957) by Alfred Hitchcock
The Bridge on the River Kwai (1957) by David Lean
Twelve Angry Men (1957) by Sidney Lumet
Witness for the Prosecution (1957) by Billy Wilder
Vertigo (1958) by Alfred Hitchcock

Cat on a Hot Tin Roof (1958) by Richard Brooks
A Night to Remember (1958) by Roy Baker
Touch of Evil (1958) by Orson Welles
Plan Nine from Outer Space (1959) by Edward D. Wood, Jr.
Ben Hur (1959) by William Wyler
Suddenly Last Summer (1959) by Joseph L. Mankiewicz
North By Northwest (1959) by Alfred Hitchcock
Shadows (1959) by John Cassavetes
On the Beach (1959) by Stanley Kramer
Anatomy of a Murder (1959) by Otto Preminger
Some Like It Hot (1959) by Billy Wilder
Spartacus (1960) by Stanley Kubrick
The Apartment (1960) by Billy Wilder
Inherit the Wind (1960) by Stanley Kramer
Psycho (1960) by Alfred Hitchcock
The Misfits (1961) by John Huston
Lawrence of Arabia (1962) by David Lean
Long Day's Journey Into Night (1962) by Sidney Lumet
To Kill a Mockingbird (1962) by Robert Mulligan
The Manchurian Candidate (1962) by John Frankenheimer
West Side Story (1962) by Robert Wise
Cleopatra (1963) by Joseph L. Mankiewicz
The Birds (1963) by Alfred Hitchcock
Hud (1963) by Martin Ritt
Dr. Strangelove (1964) by Stanley Kubrick
My Fair Lady (1964) by George Cukor
Dog Star Man (1964) by Stanley Brakhage
The Sound of Music (1965) by Robert Wise
Who's Afraid of Virginia Woolf? (1966) by Mike Nichols
A Man for All Seasons (1966) by Fred Zinnemann
What's Up Tiger Lily (1966) by Woody Allen
Titicut Follies (1967) by Frederick Wiseman
In Cold Blood (1967) by Richard Brooks
The Graduate (1967) by Mike Nichols
Don't Look Back (1967) by D. A. Pennebaker
Bonnie and Clyde (1967) by Arthur Penn
Portrait of Jason (1967) by Shirley Clarke
Chimes at Midnight (1967) by Orson Welles
Cool Hand Luke (1967) by Stuart Rosenberg
The Producers (1968) by Mel Brooks
Planet of the Apes (1968) by Franklin Schaffner
Oliver (1968) by Carol Reed

2001: A Space Odyssey (1968) by Stanley Kubrick
Take the Money and Run (1969) by Woody Allen
Easy Rider (1969) by Dennis Hopper
Midnight Cowboy (1969) by John Schlesinger
The Wild Bunch (1969) by Sam Peckinpah
M*A*S*H (1970) by Robert Altman
Patton (1970) by Franklin Schaffner
Little Big Man (1970) by Arthur Penn
Frenzy (1972) by Alfred Hitchcock
The Godfather (1972) by Francis Ford Coppola
Everything You Always Wanted to Know About Sex (1972) by Woody
    Allen
Cabaret (1972) by Bob Fosse
Last Tango in Paris (1973) by Bernardo Bertolucci
The Long Goodbye (1973) by Robert Altman
Chinatown (1974) by Roman Polanski
Young Frankenstein (1974) by Mel Brooks
Love and Death (1975) by Woody Allen
Nashville (1975) by Robert Altman
One Flew Over the Cuckoo's Nest (1975) by Milos Forman
Taxi Driver (1976) by Martin Scorsese
Network (1976) by Sidney Lumet
The Front (1976) by Martin Ritt
All the President's Men (1976) by Alan Pakula
Annie Hall (1977) by Woody Allen
Eraserhead (1977) by David Lynch
Interiors (1978) by Woody Allen
Gates of Heaven (1978) by Errol Morris
Days of Heaven (1978) by Terrence Malick
Apocalypse Now (1979) by Francis Ford Coppola
Being There (1979) by Hal Ashby
Manhattan (1979) by Woody Allen
The Elephant Man (1980) by David Lynch
Raging Bull (1980) by Martin Scorsese
Altered States (1980) by Ken Russell
On Golden Pond (1981) by Mark Rydell
Reds (1981) by Warren Beatty
Vernon, Florida (1981) by Errol Morris
My Dinner with André (1982) by Louis Malle
Blade Runner (1982) by Ridley Scott
Tootsie (1982) by Sydney Pollack
Gandhi (1982) by Richard Attenborough

Koyaanisqatsi (1983) by Godfrey Reggio
Zelig (1983) by Woody Allen
This is Spinal Tap (1984) by Rob Reiner
Once Upon a Time in the West (1984) by Sergio Leone
Amadeus (1984) by Milos Forman
Stranger Than Paradise (1984) by Jim Jarmusch
Brazil (1985) by Terry Gilliam
Down By Law (1986) by Jim Jarmusch
Platoon (1986) by Oliver Stone
Blue Velvet (1986) by David Lynch
Hannah and Her Sisters (1986) by Woody Allen
Matewan (1987) by John Sayles
House of Games (1987) by David Mamet
The Unbearable Lightness of Being (1987) by Philip Kaufman
Full Metal Jacket (1987) by Stanley Kubrick
Gorillas in the Mist (1988) by Michael Apted
The Thin Blue Line (1988) by Errol Morris
sex, lies, & videotape (1989) by Steven Soderbergh
Do the Right Thing (1989) by Spike Lee
Mystery Train (1989) by Jim Jarmusch
Henry V (1989) by Kenneth Branagh
Crimes and Misdemeanors (1989) by Woody Allen
Roger and Me (1989) by Michael Moore
The Unbelievable Truth (1989) by Hal Hartley
Awakenings (1990) by Penny Marshall
Mindwalk (1990) by Bernt Capra
Trust (1990) by Hal Hartley
Hearts of Darkness (1991) by Fax Bahr and George Hickenlooper
JFK (1991) by Oliver Stone
Thelma and Louise (1991) by Ridley Scott
Barton Fink (1991) by Joel and Ethan Coen
Night on Earth (1991) by Jim Jarmusch
Blood in the Face (1991) by Anne Bohlen, Kevin Rafferty, James
    Ridgeway
Boyz N the Hood (1991) by John Singleton
Shadows and Fog (1992) by Woody Allen
Brother's Keeper (1992) by Joe Berlinger and Bruce Sinofsky
The Player (1992) by Robert Altman
Visions of Light (1992) by Arnold Glassman, Todd McCarthy, Stuart
    Samuels
Schindler's List (1994) by Steven Spielberg
Crumb (1995) by Terry Zwigoff

Living in Oblivion (1995) by Tom DiCillo
Theremin (1995) by Steven M. Martin
Paradise Lost (1996) by Joe Berlinger and Bruce Sinofsky
Fargo (1996) by Joel and Ethan Coen
Smoke (1996) by Wayne Wang
Flirt (1996) by Hal Hartley
Lone Star (1996) by John Sayles
From the Journals of Jean Seberg (1996) by Mark Rappaport
Dead Man (1996) by Jim Jarmusch
Fast, Cheap, & Out of Control (1997) by Errol Morris
In the Company of Men (1997) by Neil LaBute
Deconstructing Harry (1997) by Woody Allen
Buffalo 66 (1998) by Vincent Gallo
Henry Fool (1998) by Hal Hartley
Zero Effect (1998) by Jake Kasdan
Your Friends and Neighbors (1998) by Neil LaBute
Pi (1998) by Darren Aronofsky
Celebrity (1998) by Woody Allen
Limbo (1999) by John Sayles
Cradle Will Rock (1999) by Tim Robbins
The Straight Story (1999) by David Lynch
Ghost Dog: The Way of the Samurai (1999) by Jim Jarmusch
Mr. Death: The Rise and Fall of Fred A. Leuchter, Jr. (1999) by Errol
    Morris
Julien Donkey-Boy (1999) by Harmony Korine
Time Code (2000) by Mike Figgis

Appendix D

IMPORTANT FOREIGN FILMS

A Trip to the Moon (France, 1902) by Georges Méliès
The Student of Prague (Ger., 1912) by Stellan Rye
Cabiria (Italy, 1914) by Giovanni Pastrone
The Outlaw and His Wife (Sweden, 1917) by Victor Sjöström
J'Accuse (France, 1919) by Abel Gance
The Cabinet of Dr. Caligari (Ger., 1919) by Robert Wiene
The Golem [*Der Golem*] (Ger., 1920) by Paul Wegener
Destiny (Ger., 1921) by Fritz Lang
Dr. Mabuse, the Gambler (Ger., 1922) by Fritz Lang
Nosferatu (Ger., 1922) by F. W. Murnau
Return to Reason (France, 1923) by Man Ray
Symphonie Diagonale [*Diagonal Symphony*] (Ger., 1924) by Viking
    Eggeling
Entre'acte (France, 1924) by René Clair
Ballet Mecanique (France, 1924) by Fernand Leger
Strike (Russia, 1924) by Sergei Eisenstein
The Last Laugh (Ger., 1924) by F. W. Murnau
Die Nibelungen [*Siegfried* and *Kriemhild's Revenge*] (Ger., 1924) by
    Fritz Lang
Battleship Potemkin (Russia, 1925) by Sergei Eisenstein
Joyless Street (Ger., 1925) by G. W. Pabst
Faust (Ger., 1926) by F. W. Murnau
Mother (Russia, 1926) by Vserolod Pudovkin
Metropolis (Ger., 1926) by Fritz Lang
Diary of a Lost Girl (Ger., 1926) by G. W. Pabst
Napoleon (France, 1927) by Abel Gance
Berlin, Symphony of a Great City (Ger., 1927) by Walter Ruttman
The Student of Prague (Ger., 1927) by Henrik Galeen
Ten Days That Shook the World [AKA: *October*] (USSR, 1928) by
    Sergei Eisenstein
Passion of Joan of Arc (France, 1928) by Carl Theodore Dreyer
The Man with the Movie Camera (Russia, 1928) by Dziga Vertov
Pandora's Box (Ger., 1928) by G. W. Pabst
Un Chien Andalou (Spain, 1929) by Luis Buñuel

L'Age D'Or [*Age of Gold*] (France, 1930) by Luis Buñuel
The Blue Angel (Ger., 1930) by Josef von Sternberg
Earth (USSR, 1930) by Alexander Dovzhenko
The Blood of a Poet (France, 1930) by Jean Cocteau
Maedchen in Uniform (Ger., 1931) by Leontine Sagan
M (Ger., 1931) by Fritz Lang
A Nous la Liberte (France, 1931) by René Clair
Vampyr (Ger., 1932) by Carl Theodore Dreyer
The Testament of Dr. Mabuse (Ger., 1932) by Fritz Lang
Ecstasy (CZ, 1933) by Gustav Machaty
Zero for Conduct (France, 1933) by Jean Vigo
L'Atalante (France, 1934) by Jean Vigo
Triumph of the Will (Ger., 1935) by Leni Riefenstahl
A Day in the Country (France, 1936) by Jean Renoir
Things to Come (G. B., 1936) by William Cameron
Grand Illusion (France, 1937) by Jean Renoir
La Bête Humaine (France, 1938) by Jean Renoir
J'Accuse (France, 1938) by Abel Gance
Alexander Nevsky (USSR, 1938) by Sergei Eisenstein
Story of the Last Chrysanthemum (Japan, 1939) by Kenji Mizoguchi
Rules of the Game (France, 1939) by Jean Renoir
Ossessione (Italy, 1942) by Luchino Visconti
Baron Munchausen (Ger., 1943) by Josef von Baky
Ivan the Terrible, Part I (USSR, 1945) by Sergei Eisenstein
Children of Paradise (France, 1945) by Marcel Carne
Open City (Italy, 1945) by Roberto Rossellini
Brief Encounter (G. B., 1946) by David Lean
La Belle et la Bête [*Beauty and the Beast*] (France, 1946) by Jean
    Cocteau
Paisan (Italy, 1946) by Roberto Rossellini
Amore (Italy, 1948) by Roberto Rossellini
The Bicycle Thief (Italy, 1948) by Vittorio De Sica
Les Enfants Terribles (France, 1949) by Jean-Pierre Melville
Orpheus (France, 1949) by Jean Cocteau
La Ronde (France, 1950) by Max Ophuls
Los Olvidados (Mexico, 1950) by Luis Buñuel
Rashomon (Japan, 1950) by Akira Kurosawa
Life of Oharu (Japan, 1952) by Kenji Mizoguchi
Ikuru (Japan, 1952) by Akira Kurosawa
Forbidden Games (France, 1952) by René Clement
An Autumn Afternoon (Japan, 1952) by Yasujiro Ozu
Ugetsu (Japan, 1953) by Kenji Mizoguchi

Tokyo Story (Japan, 1953) by Yasujiro Ozu
La Strada (Italy, 1954) by Federico Fellini
The Seven Samurai (Japan, 1954) by Akira Kurosawa
Chikamatsu Monogatari [Crucified Lovers] (Japan, 1954) by Kenji Mizoguchi
Pather Panchali (India, 1955) by Satyajit Ray
Lola Montes (France./Ger., 1955) by Max Ophuls
The Wages of Fear (France, 1955) by Henri-Georges Clouzet
Diabolique (France, 1955) by Henri-Georges Clouzot
The Red Balloon (France, 1955) by Pascal Lamorisse
Umberto D (Italy, 1955) by Vittorio De Sica
Night and Fog (France, 1955) by Alain Resnais
Senso (Italy, 1955) by Luchino Visconti
Bob le Flambeur (France, 1955) by Jean-Pierre Melville
The Mystery of Picasso (France, 1956) by Henri-Georges Clouzet
Throne of Blood (Japan, 1957) by Akira Kurosawa
The Cranes Are Flying (USSR, 1957) by Mikhail Kalatozov
Wild Strawberries (Sweden, 1957) by Ingmar Bergman
Nights of Cabiria (Italy, 1957) by Federico Fellini
The Seventh Seal (Sweden, 1957) by Ingmar Bergman
Aparajito (India, 1957) by Satyajit Ray
Ivan the Terrible, Part II (USSR, 1958) by Sergei Eisenstein
A Night to Remember (G. B., 1958) by Roy Baker
Le Beau Serge (France, 1958) by Claude Chabrol
Ashes and Diamonds (Pol., 1958) by Andrzej Wajda
Black Orpheus (Brazil, 1958) by Marcel Camus
Hiroshima, mon Amour (France, 1959) by Alain Resnais
Breathless (France, 1959) by Jean-Luc Godard
The 400 Blows (France, 1959) by François Truffaut
The World of Apu (India, 1959) by Satyajit Ray
Floating Weeds (Japan, 1959) by Yasujiro Ozu
The Testament of Orpheus (France, 1959) by Jean Cocteau
L'Avventura (Italy, 1960) by Michelangelo Antonioni
Shoot the Piano Player (France, 1960) by François Truffaut
The Lady with the Dog (USSR, 1960) by Iosif Kheyfits
The Virgin Spring (Sweden, 1960) by Ingmar Bergman
La Dolce Vita (Italy, 1960) by Federico Fellini
Peeping Tom (G. B., 1960) by Michael Powell
Mouchette (France, 1960) by Robert Bresson
Through a Glass Darkly (Sweden, 1961) by Ingmar Bergman
The Sky Above, the Mud Below (France, 1961) by Pierre-Dominique Gaisseau

Yojimbo (Japan, 1961) by Akira Kurosawa
Last Year at Marienbad (France, 1961) by Alain Resnais
La Notte (Italy, 1961) by Michelangelo Antonioni
Cleo from 5 to 7 (France/Italy, 1961) by Agnes Varda
Viridiana (Spain, 1961) by Luis Buñuel
My Life to Live (France, 1962) by Jean-Luc Godard
Knife in the Water (Pol., 1962) by Roman Polanski
La Jetée (France, 1962) by Chris Marker
Sundays and Cybele (Fr., 1962) by Serge Bourguignon
Jules and Jim (France, 1962) by François Truffaut
The Exterminating Angel (Mex., 1962) by Luis Buñuel
Contempt (France, 1963) by Jean-Luc Godard
Mondo Cane (Italy, 1963) by Gualtiero Jacopetti
8 1/2 (Italy, 1963) by Federico Fellini
The Silence (Sweden, 1963) by Ingmar Bergman
Winter Light (Sweden, 1963) by Ingmar Bergman
Red Desert (Italy, 1964) by Michelangelo Antonioni
A Hard Days Night (G. B., 1964) by Richard Lester
Woman in the Dunes (Japan, 1964) by Hiroshi Teshigahara
Band of Outsiders (France, 1964) by Jean-Luc Godard
The Umbrellas of Cherbourg (Framce/Ger., 1964) by Jacques Demy
Repulsion (G. B., 1965) by Roman Polanski
Loves of a Blonde (CZ, 1965) by Milos Forman
Le Bonheur (France, 1965) by Agnes Varda
The Round-Up (Hungary, 1965) by Miklos Jancso
Pierrot le Fou (France, 1965) by Jean-Luc Godard
Alphaville (France, 1965) by Jean-Luc Godard
Persona (Sweden, 1966) by Ingmar Bergman
Blow-Up (G. B./Italy, 1966) by Michelangelo Antonioni
Closely Watched Trains (CZ, 1966) by Jiri Menzel
L'Eclisse [*The Eclipse*] (Italy, 1966) by Michelangelo Antonioni
Masculin Feminin (France, 1966) by Jean-Luc Godard
Mouchette (France, 1966) by Robert Bresson
Andrei Rublev (USSR, 1966) by Andrei Tarkovsky
Death of a Bureaucrat (Cuba, 1966) by Tomas Gutierrez Alea
Weekend (France, 1967) by Jean-Luc Godard
Firemen's Ball (CZ, 1967) by Milos Forman
Belle de Jour (France, 1967) by Luis Buñuel
Hour of the Wolf (Sweden, 1968) by Ingmar Bergman
Yellow Submarine (G. B., 1968) by George Dunning
Le Boucher (France/Italy, 1969) by Claude Chabrol
Fellini Satyricon (Italy, 1969) by Federico Fellini

Z (France, 1969) by Constantin Costa-Gavras
Decameron (Italy, 1970) by Paolo Pasolini
Even Dwarfs Started Small (Ger., 1970) by Werner Herzog
The Conformist (Italy, 1970) by Bernardo Bertolucci
The Sorrow and the Pity (France/Switz./Ger., 1970) by Marcel Ophuls
Tristiana (France/Italy/Spain, 1970) by Luis Buñuel
In the Realm of the Senses (Japan, 1971) by Nagisa Oshima
Clair's Knee (France, 1971) by Eric Rohmer
Murmur of the Heart (France, 1971) by Louis Malle
The Garden of the Finzi-Continis (Italy, 1971) by Vittorio De Sica
Man of Marble (Pol., 1972) by Andrzej Wajda
Cries and Whispers (Sweden, 1972) by Ingmar Bergman
The Discreet Charm of the Bourgeoisie (France, 1972) by Luis Buñuel
Aguirre: The Wrath of God (Ger., 1972) by Werner Herzog
Last Tango in Paris (Italy/France, 1972) by Bernardo Bertolucci
Spirit of the Beehive (Spain, 1973) by Victor Erice
The Magic Flute (Sweden, 1973) by Ingmar Bergman
Day for Night (France, 1973) by François Truffaut
Phantom of Liberty (France, 1974) by Luis Buñuel
The Mystery of Kaspar Hauser (Ger., 1974) by Werner Herzog
Dersu Uzala (USSR/Japan, 1974) by Akira Kurosawa
Effi Briest (Ger., 1974) by Rainer Werner Fassbinder
Amarcord (Italy, 1974) by Federico Fellini
Face to Face (Sweden, 1975) by Ingmar Bergman
Swept Away (Italy, 1975) by Lina Wertmuller
Monty Python and the Holy Grail (G. B., 1975) by Terry Gilliam
Seven Beauties (Italy, 1975) by Lina Wertmuller
The Man Who Fell to Earth (G. B., 1976) by Nicolas Roeg
Peppermint Soda (France, 1977) by Diane Kurys
That Obscure Object of Desire (Spain/France, 1977) by Luis Buñuel
Man of Marble (Pol., 1977) by Andrzej Wajda
Autumn Sonata (Sweden, 1978) by Ingmar Bergman
Portrait of Teresa (Cuba, 1979) by Pastor Vega
The Tin Drum (Ger., 1979) by Volker Schlondorff
The Marriage of Maria Braun (Ger., 1979) by Rainer Werner
   Fassbinder
Kagemusha (Japan, 1980) by Akira Kurosawa
Das Boot (Ger., 1981) by Wolfgang Petersen
Dimensions of Dialogue (CZ, 1982) by Jan Svankmajer
Fitzcarraldo (Ger., 1982) by Werner Herzog
Man of Iron (Pol., 1982) by Andrzej Wajda
Yol (Turkey, 1982) by Serif Goren

The Road Warrior (Australia, 1982) by George Miller
Fanny and Alexander (Sweden, 1983) by Ingmar Bergman
Berlin Alexanderplatz (Ger., 1983) by Rainer Werner Fassbinder
L'Argent (France/Switz., 1983) by Robert Bresson
Yellow Earth (1984) by Chen Kaige
Sheer Madness (Ger./France, 1985) by Margarethe von Trotta
Shoah (France, 1985) by Claude Lanzman
Ran (Japan, 1985) by Akira Kurosawa
Men (Ger., 1985) by Doris Dörrie
Man Facing Southeast (Argentina, 1986) by Eliseo Subiela
Babette's Feast (Denmark, 1987) by Gabriel Axel
Jean de Florette (France, 1987) by Claude Berri
Manon of the Spring (France, 1987) by Claude Berri
Tampopo (Japan, 1987) by Juzo Itami
Wings of Desire (Ger., 1987) by Wim Wenders
My Life as a Dog (Sweden, 1987) by Lasse Hallstrom
Au Revoir les Enfants (France, 1988) by Louis Malle
Pelle the Conqueror (Denmark, 1988) by Billie August
The Cook, the Thief, His Wife and Her Lover (G. B./France, 1989) by
    Peter Greenaway
My Left Foot (Ireland, 1989) by Jim Sheridan
Sweetie (Australia, 1989) by Jane Campion
Ju Dou (China/Japan, 1989) by Zhang Yimou
Cinema Paradiso (Italy, 1989) by Giuseppe Tomatore
Journey of Hope (Switz., 1990) by Xavier Koller
High Heels (Spain, 1990) by Pedro Almodovar
Tale of Springtime (France, 1990) by Eric Rohmer
Dreams (Japan, 1990) by Akira Kurosawa
Time of the Gypsies (Yugoslavia, 1990) by Emir Kusterica
The Double Life of Veronique (Pol./France, 1991) by Krzysztof
    Kieslowski
Raise the Red Lantern (China/Taiwan, 1991) by Zhang Yimou
The Nasty Girl (Ger., 1991) by Michael Verhoeven
Zentropa (Denmark, 1991) by Lars von Trier
Europa Europa (Pol./France, 1991) by Agnieska Holland
Prospero's Books (G. B., 1991) by Peter Greenaway
Mediterraneo (Italy, 1991) by Gabriele Salvatores
Delicatessen (France, 1991) by Jean-Marie Jeunet and Marc Caro
The Lovers on the Bridge (France, 1991) by Léos Carax
Latcho Drom [Safe Journey] (France, 1992) by Tony Gatlif
Life and Nothing More (Iran, 1992) by Abbas Kiarostami

Like Water for Chocolate (Mex., 1992) by Alfonso Arau
Ciao, Professore (Italy, 1993) by Lina Wertmuller
The Piano (Australia/NZ, 1993) by Jane Campion
Faraway, So Close (Ger., 1993) by Wim Wenders
Farewell My Concubine (China, 1993) by Chen Kaige
Blue (France, 1993) by Krzysztof Kieslowski
The Blue Kite (China, 1993) by Tian Zhuangzhuang
Red (Switz./France, 1994) by Krzysztof Kieslowski
Lisbon Story (Ger./Portugal, 1994) by Wim Wenders
Heavenly Creatures (NZ, 1994) by Peter Jackson
To Live (China, 1994) by Zhang Yimou
Naked (G. B., 1994) by Mike Leigh
Caro Diario (Italy, 1994) by Nanni Moretti
Il Postino [*The Postman*] (Italy, 1995) by Michael Radford
Underground (France/Ger./Hungary, 1995) by Emir Kusterica
Maborosi (Japan, 1995) by Hirokazu Kore-eda
Lamerica (Italy, 1995) by Gianni Amelio
The City of Lost Children (France, 1995) by Marc Caro and Jean-Pierre
    Jeunet
Lessons of Darkness (Ger., 1995) by Werner Herzog
Secrets and Lies (G. B., 1996) by Mike Leigh
Breaking the Waves (Denmark, 1996) by Lars von Trier
Chungking Express (Hong Kong, 1996) by Wong Kar-Wai
Winter Sleepers (Ger., 1997) by Tom Tykwer
The Sweet Hereafter (Canada, 1997) by Atom Egoyan
Taste of Cherry (Iran, 1997) by Abbas Kiarostami
Junk Mail (Norway, 1997) by Pål Sletaune
The Pillow Book (G. B., 1997) by Peter Greenaway
Little Dieter Needs to Fly (Ger., 1997) by Werner Herzog
Life is Beautiful (Italy, 1998) by Roberto Benigni
The Idiots (Denmark, 1998) by Lars von Trier
The Celebration (Denmark, 1998) by Thomas Vinterberg
Autumn Tale (France, 1998) by Eric Rohmer
Last Night (Canada, 1998) by Don McKellar
Run Lola Run (Ger., 1998) by Tom Tykwer
After Life (Japan, 1999) by Hirokazu Kore-eda
Tuvalu (Ger., 1999) by Veit Helmer
Harry, He's Here to Help (France, 2000) by Dominik Moll
Dancer in the Dark (Denmark, 2000) by Lars von Trier

GLOSSARY

aleatory The technique of filmmaking that uses chance as a major element in composing and filming. Often used in documentaries when scenes are photographed on the spot, without rehearsal or set up.

allegory A symbolized style in which the situation and objects used represent major themes such as death, birth, justice, etc.

archetype A model after which things are patterned. A distinctive type of personality or story. A character who is a universal representation of certain human qualities. Often used in fairy tales, myths, and epics.

aspect ratio The mathematical ratio between the horizontal size and the vertical size of the film screen. The dimensions are represented as 1.33:1 for example, which is the standard aspect ratio for older movies.

auteur theory The theory that the director of a film is like an author (French = auteur) who is responsible for the overall theme and vision of a film. The theory that a film is a personal reflection of the director's ideas. First suggested in the famous French film journal, *Cahiers du Cinema,* in the 1950s.

avant-garde Those people and ideas that are in the forefront of a movement, particularly in the arts. The experimental filmmakers who use atypical, unusual, daring, and often intellectual methods and ideas about filmmaking. From the French, literally "in the front ranks."

B film A low budget movie meant to be a second feature, usually formulaic, using non-stars for actors.

bird's-eye-view A shot taken with the camera directly above the subject. Also called an overhead shot.

blocking The planned movements of the actors within a scene.

chiaroscuro The technique of using dramatic light and shadow photography effects; the arrangement of bright and dark elements in a work of art to create depth or drama; the creation of black and white images and mysterious, shadowy scenes. Often used in Expressionism to elicit certain moods and create visual highlights.

cinematography The lighting, focusing, use of filters, camera movement and angles, and other photographic elements involved in film-making. Everything involving the camera.

cinema vérité An approach to nonfiction filmmaking in which the camera simply records events without interference and without narration. From the French, literally "film truth."

classical cinema Mainstream films, usually from Hollywood, that use a standard approach to cinema—a movie star, a simple story with drama, tension, and climax, using conventional techniques, etc.

cognition All mental and intellectual processes of the brain and mind including memory, perception, reasoning, and thinking.

Dada (Dadaism) An art movement that began after World War I that stressed nonsense, irrationality, and irreverence. Artists were angry that rational thinking could not stop the war so they turned to irrational, absurd, spontaneous, and mocking art.

day-for-night Filming during the daytime using special filters on the cameras to give the impression that it is nighttime.

deep focus A photographic technique that allows for the people and objects far away from the camera as well as those close to the camera to be in focus at the same time.

denouement The final disposition or climax of a story, or the period of calm immediately after the climax.

depth of field A photographic term that refers to the range of focus in an image. The distance within which objects are in focus.

diegesis The total world of events, actions, and sounds that are part of the story in a narrative film. Nondiegetic elements such as music are outside of the plot or story.

dissolve The slow fading out of one image and the gradual fading in of another usually with a superimposition in-between.

documentary A nonfiction film using non-actors to show real events and people. Defined as "the creative treatment of actuality."

dubbing Adding sound to a film after the visual images have already been photographed. From the term "double." Usually refers to actors' voices in another language substituting for the original language.

Dutch angle A shot in which the camera angle is oblique or diagonal.

epic A film genre with bold, universal themes, usually treating historical topics, with spectacular scenes and costumes, heroes, long time-frames, cultural values, and sweeping moral topics.

Expressionism An approach to art that emphasizes style and symbolism instead of Realism. Often includes the artist's emotional expression of ideas and beliefs. Is meant to evoke feelings through universal, symbolic images and sounds by distorting reality.

film noir A film genre emphasizing fatalistic, despairing, paranoid human relationships. Usually includes urban life, crime, deception, and ultimately death. A hard-boiled hero meets a beautiful, but cold-hearted woman. Popular in the 1940s and 50s, the term was coined by the French and means "black cinema." The lighting is shadowy, dark, high contrast, and usually interior (coming from within the scene).

Formalism An approach to film emphasizing beauty and style over realism or subject matter. Often poetic or experimental, the focus is on the form of images rather than on the story.

genre A certain type or category of films, such as western, crime, sci-fi, horror, film noir, romantic comedy, thriller, etc.

homage A respectful tribute to a person, style, or movie made as a reference, sometimes indirect, within a work of art.

HUAC The House Un-American Activities Committee during the 1950s led by Senator Joseph McCarthy that attempted to root out Communists from U.S. society and succeeded in preventing many film artists from working in the movie industry.

iconography The pictorial material used to illustrate or suggest a subject; the conventional visual images associated with a subject, or the imagery used in a work of art.

intertitles Words put on the screen between images during a silent film to help explain the story or tell what the characters are saying.

irony A literary or dramatic technique that involves opposites, contrasts, incongruity, or unexpected events that are amusing or meaningful because of their juxtaposition.

kinetic A term from the ancient Greek that refers to movement; Source of the term "cinema."

Kinetoscope An early film-viewing machine, a four-feet high box that used a short loop of film which could be viewed by one person at a time looking through an opening in the top.

letterbox The style of a television view of a film that uses the original aspect ratio of the film so the images are kept in the same proportions as in the original film. Typically involves masking the top and bottom of the television screen.

lyrical Poetic, beautiful, fun, exuberant, light-hearted, producing emotion.

masking A technique of blocking out a portion of the screen so as to change the aspect ratio and perhaps draw attention to certain images or to intensify the aesthetics.

Minimalism An artistic approach that stresses the concept that "less is more." Uses restraint, austerity, quiet, and slow pacing.

mise-en-scene The arrangement of people and objects within the visual space or on the stage. Involves establishing the placement of people and objects, planning the movement, action, and the photographic angles and focusing. Usually the film director makes the final decisions regarding these elements.

montage Images are edited together into a rapid sequence that conveys a particular set of actions and feelings. Part of the editing process —but refers to a particular sequence of visuals in one scene and the way they are put together.

motif An idea, theme, or symbolic concept that is repeated throughout a film giving the film a central focus.

narrative A film that tells a story, has a plot, as in nearly all fictional films and most nonfiction films.

Neorealism An artistic film movement that began in Italy in the 1940s and attempted to portray real, ordinary people and strong emotions. Often centered on social problems, location settings, and non-actors.

New Wave A film movement in France in the 1950s-60s that emphasized the director as the main influence on the character of a film and argued that film should not follow literature but should use improvisation and intellectually and emotionally genuine themes.

non-narrative A film that does not tell a story, has no plot—most often seen in experimental films and only occassionaly in main feature films, such as *Koyaanisqatsi* (1983).

oeuvre The complete body of work of an artist considered as a whole.

pan (panning) The horizontal movement of a camera; short for "panorama."

persistence of vision The physiological process whereby the eye retains an image for a split second after the stimulus is gone. One of the perceptual processes that allows us to perceive continuous motion from a series of rapidly presented still images.

POV (point-of-view) shot The camera angle gives the impression that we are seeing what a character is seeing.

proscenium The typical, common theater arrangement with the audience all facing one way toward a stage with curtain and archway. Film showings mimic the theater's proscenium style, as opposed to theater-in-the-round or the thrust style of stage.

proxemics The distances and spatial relationships between characters and objects within the mise-en-scene.

rack focus A shift in the focus of the camera during a shot meant to direct a viewer's attention to another image on the screen.

reaction shot The camera shot of a character (usually a face) showing a reaction to something that has happened.

Realism A type of film style that tries to duplicate real life. The emphasis is on common locations, themes, authentic-looking objects and sets, and no distortions.

semiotics (semiology)   An analytical approach that attempts to find meanings in signs and symbols. A theory that the arts and society are full of signs that contain a "language" with certain meanings.

social realism   A general term for films that deal with society and its flaws, often featuring the lives of ordinary people who are caught up in social and cultural problems.

shot   A piece of film that has not been edited. One take of the camera without interruption. Turn camera on, turn camera off = a shot.

storyboard   A set of sketches, like a comic strip, that outlines a film's shots before they are photographed in order to help the director and cinematographer plan the mise-en-scene.

subtext   A literary term that refers to the ideas and concerns alluded to or implied beneath the actual words and scenes.

Surrealism   An artistic and literary philosophy and art movement based on Freud's idea of the unconscious mind; it stresses that art should attempt to reveal the secrets of the unconscious.   Often irrational, absurd, nonsensical, and dream-like.

tilting   The up and down movement of the camera.

thematic montage   Weaving together different stories or themes within a film.

tinting   The coloring of filmstock. Used on black and white films to express mood or visual interest by giving color to backgrounds.

titles   Words on cards shown during silent films to explain a setting, express dialogue, or set a mood.

verisimilitude   The quality of appearing to the eye to be true or real; the extent to which an artistic image or representation looks the same as the actual object; a measure of realism in iconograpy, in look.

wipe   An editing technique that "sweeps" one image off the screen and replaces it with another, usually by using a solid line, either horizontal or vertical, that moves across the screen taking out one shot and adding the next.

BIBLIOGRAPHY

Agee, James (1967) *Agee On Film*, 2 volumes. New York: Grosset & Dunlap.

Andrew, J. Dudley. (1976) *The Major Film Theories: An Introduction*. New York: Oxford University Press.

Andrew, J. Dudley. (1984) *Concepts in Film Theory*. New York: Oxford University Press.

Anton, Ferdinand, et. al. (1979) *Primitive Art*. New York: Abrams.

Arakawa & Gins, Madeline H. (1979) *The Mechanism of Meaning*. New York: Abrams.

Arnason, H. Harvard. (1977) *History of Modern Art*. New York: Abrams.

Arnheim, Rudolf. (1957) *Film as Art*. Berkeley: University of California Press.

Ashton, Dore. (1969) *A Reading of Modern Art*. Cleveland: Case Western University Press.

Balio, Tino. (1993) *Grand Design: Hollywood as a Modern Business Enterprise, 1930-1939*, volume 5 in *History of the American Cinema*. New York: Charles Scribner's Sons.

Barnouw, Dagmar. (1994) *Critical Realism: History, Photography, and the Work of Sidgfried Kracauer*. Baltimore and London: The Johns Hopkins University Press.

Bazin, André. (1967) *What is Cinema?* Berkeley: University of California Press.

Bergman, Ingmar. (1967) *A Film Trilogy*. New York: Orion Press.

Bergman, Ingmar. (1988) *The Magic Lantern: An Autobiography*. New York: Penguin Books.

Bordwell, David. (1985) *Narration in the Fiction Film*. Madison: University of Wisconsin Press.

Bordwell, David. (1989) *Making Meaning: Inference and Rhetoric in the Interpretation of Cinema*. Cambridge, MA: Harvard University Press.

Bordwell, David. (1997) *On the History of Film Style*. Cambridge, MA: Harvard University Press.

Bordwell, David & Carroll, Noel, eds. (1996) *Post-Theory: Reconstructing Film Studies*. Madison: University of Wisconsin Press.

Bowser, Eileen. (1990) *The Transformation of Cinema: 1907-1915*, volume 2 in *History of the American Cinema*. New York: Charles Scribner's Sons.

Cage, John. (1993) *John Cage: Writer*. Edited by Richard Kostelanetz. New York: Proscenium Publishers.

Canady, John. (1980) *What is Art?* New York: Alfred A. Knopf.

Carroll, Noel. (1988) *Mystifying Movies: Fads and Fallacies in Contemporary Film Theory*. New York: Columbia University Press.

Carroll, Noel. (1988) *Philosophical Problems of Classical Film Theory*. Princeton, NJ: Princeton University Press.

Casty, Alan. (1973) *Development of the Film: An Interpretive History*. New York: Harcourt, Brace, Jovanovich.

Cook, David. (1996) *A History of Narrative Film*, 3rd edition. New York: Norton.

Crafton, Donald. (1997) *The Talkies: American Cinema's Transition to Sound, 1926-1931*, volume 4 in *History of the American Cinema*. New York: Charles Scribner's Sons.

Dancyger, Ken. (1999) *The World of Film and Video Production*. New York: Harcourt Brace.

Danto, Arthur C. (1993) "State of the Art." *Artforum,* Special issue, September, p. 128.

DelaCroix, Horst & Tansey, Richard G. (1986) *Art Through the Ages*, 7th edition. New York: Harcourt, Brace, Jovanovich.

DeNitto, Dennis & Herman, William. (1975) *Film and the Critical Eye*. New York: Macmillan.

D'Harnoncourt, Anne. (1973) *Marcel Duchamp*. New York: Museum of Modern Art.

Dwoskin, Stephen. (1985) *Film Is: The International Free Cinema*. Woodstock, NY: The Overlook Press.

Eisenstein, Sergei. (1970) *Notes of a Film Director*. New York: Dover Publications.

Eisner, Lotte H. (1952) *The Haunted Screen*. Berkeley: University of California Press.

Ellis, Jack C. (1995) *A History of Film*, 4th edition. Boston: Allyn and Bacon.

Field, Richard S. (1978) *Jasper Johns: Prints, 1970-77*. Connecticut: Wesleyan University Press.

Fromm, Erich. (1968) *The Revolution of Hope*. New York: Harper & Row.

Gaugh, Harry F. (1983) *Willem de Kooning*. New York: Abbeville Press.

Giannetti, Louis. (1987) *Understanding Movies*. Englewood Cliffs, NJ: Prentice-Hall.

Golding, John. (1968) *Cubism*. Boston: Boston Book & Art Shop.

Gombrich, E. H. (1961) *Art and Illusion: A Study in the Psychology of Pictorial Representation*. Princeton, NJ: Princeton University Press.

Gombrich, E. H. (1966) *The Story of Art*. New York: Phaidon Publishers.

Gombrich, E. H. (1982) *The Image and the Eye: Further Studies in the Psychology of Pictorial Representation*. Ithaca, NY: Cornell University Press.

Grant, Barry Keith. (1986) *Film Genre Reader*. Austin: University of Texas Press.

Henault, Marie. (1980) *Stanley Kunitz*. Boston: Twayne Publishers.

Herbert, Robert L. ed. (1964) *Modern Artists on Art*. Englewood Cliffs, N.J.: Prentice-Hall.

Hill, John & Gibson, Pamela Church. (1998) *The Oxford Guide to Film Studies*. Oxford: Oxford University Press.

Joachimides, Christos M. & Rosenthal, Norman, eds. (1993) *American Art in the Twentieth Century.* London: Prestel.

Jacobs, Lewis. (1970) *The Movies as Medium*. New York: Farrar, Straus, & Giroux.

Janson, H. W. (1991) *History of Art*, 4th ed. New York: Harry N. Abrams.

Joachimides, Christos M. & Rosenthal, Norman, eds. (1993) *American Art in the Twentieth Century*. London: Prestel.

Kawin, Bruce F. (1992) *How Movies Work*. Berkeley: University of California Press.

Kepes, Gyorgy, ed. (1960) *The Visual Arts Today.* Connecticut: Wesleyan University Press.

Knight, Arthur. (1957) *The Liveliest Art*. New York: New American Library.

Koszarski, Richard. (1990) *An Evening's Entertainment: The Age of the Silent Feature Picture 1915-1928*, volume 3 in *History of the American Cinema*. New York: Charles Scribner's Sons.

Kozloff, Max. (1966) *Jasper Johns.* New York: Abrams.

Kracauer, Siegfried. (1947) *From Caligari to Hitler*. Princeton, NJ: Princeton University Press.

Lanier, Vincent. (1982) *The Arts We See*. New York: Teachers College Press.

Lehman, Peter, ed. (1997) *Defining Cinema*. New Brunswick, NJ: Rutgers University Press.

Lippard, Lucy R. (1983) *Overlay: Contemporary Art and the Art of Prehistory.* New York: Pantheon Books.

Lucie-Smith, Edward. (1972) *Symbolist Art.* New York: Praeger.

Lumet, Sidney. (1995) *Making Movies.* New York: Knopf.

Mamer, Bruce. (2000) *Film Production Technique: Creating the Accomplished Image*, 2nd edition. Belmont, CA: Wadsworth Publishing Co.

Marcus, Greil. (1989) *Lipstick Traces: A Secret History of the Twentieth Century.* Cambridge, Mass.: Harvard University Press.

McShine, Kynaston, ed. (1989) *Andy Warhol: A Retrospective.* New York: Museum of Modern Art.

Museum of Modern Art (1966) *The Object Transformed.* New York: Museum of Modern Art.

Musser, Charles. (1990) *The Emergence of Cinema: The American Screen to 1907*, volume 1 in *History of the American Cinema.* New York: Charles Scribner's Sons.

Neuman, Erich. (1959) *Art and the Creative Unconscious.* Princeton: Princeton University Press.

Nowell-Smith, Geoffrey, ed. (1996) *The Oxford History of World Cinema.* Oxford: Oxford University Press.

O'Connor, Francis V. (1967) *Jackson Pollock.* New York: Museum of Modern Art.

Parkinson, David. (1995) *History of Film.* New York: Thames and Hudson.

Phillips, Gene D. (1984) *Alfred Hitchcock.* Boston: Twayne Publishers.

Phillips, William H. (1999) *Film: An Introduction.* Boston: Bedford/St. Martin's Press.

Roethel, Hans K. (1979) *Kandinsky.* New York: Hudson Hills Press.

Rubin, William S. (1968) *Dada and Surrealist Art.* New York: Abrams.

Russel, John and Gablik, Suzi. (1969) *Pop Art Redefined.* London: Thames and Hudson.

Sanders, N.K. (1968) *Prehistoric Art in Europe*. Baltimore: Penguin Books.

Sarris, Andrew. (1968) *The American Cinema*. New York: Dutton.

Schatz, Thomas (1997) *Boom and Bust: The American Cinema in the 1940s*, volume 6 in *History of the American Cinema*. New York: Charles Scribner's Sons.

Schwartz, Paul Waldo. (1971) *Cubism*. New York: Praeger.

Shipman, David. (1982) *The Story of Cinema*. New York: St. Martin's Press.

Sieveking, Ann. (1979) *The Cave Artists*. London: Thames & Hudson.

Sklar, Robert. (1993) *Film: An International History of the Medium*. New York: Harry N. Abrams and Prentice Hall.

Spoto, Donald. (1992) *The Art of Alfred Hitchcock*. New York: Doubleday.

Steinberg, Leo. (1972) *Other Criteria: Confrontations with Twentieth Century Art*. New York: Oxford University Press.

Stone, Judy. (1997) *Eye on the World: Conversations with International Filmmakers*. Beverly Hills, CA: Silman-James Press.

Torbrugge, Walter. (1968) *Prehistoric European Art*. New York: Abrams.

Tudor, Andrew. (1974) *Theories of Film*. New York: Viking Press.

Vogel, Amos. (1974) *Film As A Subversive Art*. New York: Random House.

Vogt, Paul. (1981) *Contemporary Painting*. New York: Abrams.

Warhol, Andy. (1975) *The Philosophy of Andy Warhol: From a to b and back again*. New York: Harcourt, Brace, Jovanovich.

Yenawine, Philip. (1991) *How to Look at Modern Art*. New York: Harry N. Abrams.

Youngblood, Gene. (1970) *Expanded Cinema*. New York: E. P. Dutton & Co.

INDEX